BEST OF COUNTRY
cooking *with*
cream soup

Cooking with Cream Soup

EDITOR: Sara Lancaster
ART DIRECTOR: Gretchen Trautman
LAYOUT DESIGNERS: Emma Acevedo, Kathleen Bump
PROOFREADER: Linne Bruskewitz
CONTENT PRODUCTION SUPERVISOR: Julie Wagner
EDITORIAL ASSISTANT: Barb Czysz
INDEXER: Jean Duerst

FOOD DIRECTOR: Diane Werner RD
TEST KITCHEN MANAGER: Karen Scales
RECIPE EDITORS: Sue A. Jurack (Senior), Mary King, Christine Rukavena
RECIPE ASSET SYSTEM MANAGER: Coleen Martin
TEST KITCHEN ASSISTANT: Rita Krajcir

STUDIO PHOTOGRAPHERS: Rob Hagen (Senior), Dan Roberts, Jim Wieland, Lori Foy
SENIOR FOOD STYLIST: Sarah Thompson
FOOD STYLIST ASSISTANTS: Kaitlyn Basasie, Alynna Malson
SET STYLISTS: Jennifer Bradley Vent (Senior), Stephanie Marchese, Melissa Haberman, Dee Dee Schaefer
PHOTO STUDIO COORDINATOR: Kathleen Swaney

SENIOR EDITOR/BOOKS: Mark Hagen
CREATIVE DIRECTOR: Ardyth Cope
VICE PRESIDENT,
EXECUTIVE EDITOR/BOOKS: Heidi Reuter Lloyd
EDITOR IN CHIEF: Catherine Cassidy
PRESIDENT, FOOD & ENTERTAINING: Suzanne M. Grimes
PRESIDENT AND CHIEF EXECUTIVE OFFICER: Mary G. Berner

COVER PHOTOGRAPHY: Photographer, Dan Roberts
Food Stylist, Suzanne Breckenridge
Set Stylist, Melissa Haberman

©2008 Reiman Media Group, Inc.
5400 S. 60th St.
Greendale, WI 53129

International Standard Book Number (10):
0-89821-603-6
International Standard Book Number (13):
978-0-89821-603-5
Library of Congress Control Number:
2008923022

Pictured on front cover: Au Gratin Ham Potpie (p. 62)
Pictured on title page: Artichoke Chicken (p. 68)
Pictured above left: Dijon Mushroom Beef (p. 37)
Pictured on back cover: Sausage Rice Casserole (p. 58), Broccoli Chicken Cups (p. 6), Sour Cream 'n' Dill Chicken (p. 72), Simple Mushroom Stew (p. 40) and Chicken Saltimbocca (p. 80)

Open a Can Of Possibilities!

What can you make with a can of cream soup? Green Bean Casserole? Definitely. But how about adding canned soup to oven-baked entrees, skillet recipes, side dishes, party starters and even brunch specialties? It's never been easier to lend comforting flavor and creamy richness to family staples than with *Best of Country…Cooking with Cream Soup.*

Within the pages of this mouth-watering collection, you'll discover more than 200 enticing recipes, all featuring the shortcut ingredient—canned cream soup. From down-home classics such as Swedish Meatballs (p. 39) and Turkey Tetrazzini (p. 78) to new taste twists like Au Gratin Ham Potpie (p. 62) and Cheesy Tuna Lasagna (p. 84), you'll learn the secrets behind using cream soup to create family-pleasing fare.

This heartwarming book is organized into eight handy chapters: Snacks; Soups; Sunday Brunch; Beef & Ground Beef; Pork; Chicken & Turkey; Seafood; and Sides. Best of all, every recipe was shared by a home cook and approved by the Taste of Home Test Kitchen. With 235 recipes to choose from and gorgeous full-color photographs of most dishes, you'll find plenty of mealtime inspiration.

And while you'll appreciate how a can of cream soup cuts down on kitchen time, your entire gang will enjoy the satisfying goodness it simply stirs into so many family favorites.

BEST OF COUNTRY
cooking with cream soup

great gift!

The *Best of Country Cooking with Cream Soup* makes a great gift for those who like home-style cooking. To order additional copies, specify item number 38146 and send $15.99 (plus $4.99 shipping/processing for one book, $5.99 for two or more) to: Shop Taste of Home, Suite 174, P.O. Box 26820, Lehigh Valley, PA 18002-6820. To order by credit card, call toll-free 1-800/880-3012.

CHAPTER 1
Snacks

Cheesy Sausage Dip

CURTIS COLE • DALLAS, TEXAS

The garlic really comes through in this crowd-pleasing cheese dip. It's one of our family's all-time favorites. I serve it at nearly every gathering in a slow cooker with a basket of crunchy tortilla chips.

PREP/TOTAL TIME: 20 min.

- 1   pound ground beef
- 1   pound bulk pork sausage
- 2   tablespoons all-purpose flour
- 1   can (10-3/4 ounces) condensed cream of mushroom soup, undiluted
- 1   can (10 ounces) diced tomatoes and green chilies, undrained
- 1   medium onion, chopped
- 1   tablespoon garlic powder
- 2   pounds process cheese (Velveeta), cubed

Tortilla chips

In a large saucepan, cook beef and sausage over medium heat until no longer pink; drain. Sprinkle with flour. Stir in the soup, tomatoes, onion and garlic powder. Bring to a boil; cook and stir for 2 minutes or until thickened. Reduce heat. Stir in cheese until melted. Serve warm with tortilla chips. Refrigerate leftovers. YIELD: 8 CUPS.

Souper Joes

ERLENE CORNELIUS • SPRING CITY, TENNESSEE

It's a snap to prepare these beefed-up sandwiches that get their fast flavor from onion soup mix and shredded cheddar cheese. At around a dollar a serving, they are very economical as well.

PREP/TOTAL TIME: 15 min.

- 1   pound ground beef
- 1   can (10-3/4 ounces) condensed cream of mushroom soup, undiluted
- 1   tablespoon onion soup mix
- 1   cup (4 ounces) shredded cheddar cheese
- 8   hamburger buns, split

In a large saucepan, cook beef over medium heat until no longer pink; drain. Stir in soup and soup mix; heat through. Stir in cheese until melted. Place about 1/3 cupful on each bun. YIELD: 8 SERVINGS.

turkey turnovers

Turkey Turnovers

JULIE WAGNER • NOVI, MICHIGAN

I make this dish often after the holidays when there's leftover turkey in the refrigerator or freezer. It's full of wonderful flavor and so simple to prepare.

PREP: 15 min. **BAKE:** 30 min.

- 1   package (3 ounces) cream cheese, softened
- 1   tablespoon milk
- 1/2   cup cubed cooked turkey
- 1/2   cup cooked peas *or* vegetable of your choice
- 4   teaspoons sliced almonds
- 1   tablespoon minced fresh parsley
- 1   tablespoon finely chopped onion
- 1-1/2   teaspoons diced pimientos

Dash *each* salt, pepper and garlic powder
- 1   cup biscuit/baking mix
- 1/4   cup cold water
- 1   tablespoon butter, melted
- 1/2   to 3/4 cup condensed cream of chicken soup, undiluted *or* chicken gravy

In a mixing bowl, beat cream cheese and milk until smooth. Stir in turkey, peas, almonds, parsley, onion, pimientos, salt, pepper and garlic powder; set aside.

In a bowl, combine biscuit mix and water until a soft dough forms. On a floured surface, knead gently 5-6 times or until dough is no longer sticky. Gently roll into an 11-in. x 7-in. rectangle; cut in half. Spoon half of the turkey mixture onto each. Carefully fold pastry over filling; seal edges tightly with a fork. Brush tops with butter.

Place on a greased baking sheet. Bake at 350° for 30-35 minutes or until golden brown. Meanwhile, heat soup; serve with turnovers. YIELD: 2 TURNOVERS.

broccoli chicken cups

Broccoli Chicken Cups

MARTY KINGERY • POINT PLEASANT, WEST VIRGINIA

Frozen puff pastry makes these rich and creamy appetizers quick and easy. Sometimes, instead of chopping the tomatoes, I put a slice on top of each cup before popping them in the oven.

PREP: 15 min. **BAKE:** 25 min.

2-1/2	cups diced cooked chicken breast
1	can (10-3/4 ounces) reduced-fat reduced-sodium condensed cream of chicken soup, undiluted
1	cup frozen chopped broccoli, thawed and drained
2	small plum tomatoes, seeded and chopped
1	small carrot, grated
1	tablespoon Dijon mustard
1	garlic clove, minced
1/4	teaspoon pepper
1	sheet frozen puff pastry, thawed
1/4	cup grated Parmesan cheese

In a large bowl, combine the first eight ingredients; set aside. On a lightly floured surface, roll pastry into a 12-in. x 9-in. rectangle. Cut lengthwise into four strips and widthwise into three strips. Gently press puff pastry squares into muffin cups coated with cooking spray.

Spoon chicken mixture into pastry cups. Sprinkle with Parmesan cheese. Bake at 375° for 25-30 minutes or until golden brown. Serve warm. YIELD: 1 DOZEN.

Creamy Shrimp Mousse

ELOISE BINGENHEIMER • SALEM, OREGON

Folks will think you're spoiling them when you serve this wonderful shrimp mousse! Molded in a ring, it looks fancy even as it feeds a crowd. For an impressive presentation, place it on lettuce leaves and surround it with assorted crackers for dipping.

PREP/TOTAL TIME: 15 min.

1	can (10-3/4 ounces) condensed cream of mushroom soup, undiluted
1	package (8 ounces) cream cheese, cubed
1	cup mayonnaise
1	envelope unflavored gelatin
6	tablespoons cold water
1	can (6 ounces) small shrimp, rinsed and drained *or* 1/3 cup frozen small cooked shrimp, thawed
3/4	cup chopped onion
1/2	cup chopped celery

Lettuce leaves
Fresh parsley, optional
Assorted crackers

In a large saucepan, combine the soup, cream cheese and mayonnaise. Cook and stir over medium heat until smooth; remove from the heat; set aside.

Meanwhile, in a small saucepan, sprinkle unflavored gelatin over cold water; let stand for 1 minute. Cook and stir over low heat until the gelatin is completely dissolved.

Transfer to a large mixing bowl; cool slightly. Add the shrimp, chopped onion, chopped celery and cream cheese mixture.

Transfer to a lightly greased 6-cup mold. Cover and refrigerate for 4 hours or overnight.

Unmold onto a lettuce-lined serving plate. Garnish with parsley if desired. Serve with crackers. Refrigerate leftovers. YIELD: 5 CUPS.

Mushroom Burger Stromboli

JUDY BITZ • HOONAH, ALASKA

We live in a logging camp, and grocery stores are far away. So I do a lot of baking from scratch. Slices of this stromboli taste just like a mushroom burger.

PREP: 30 min. + rising **BAKE:** 30 min.

1	package (1/4 ounce) active dry yeast
2-1/2	cups warm water (110° to 115°)
2	tablespoons vegetable oil
2	tablespoons salt
2	teaspoons sugar
7	to 7-1/2 cups all-purpose flour
1	pound ground beef
1/4	cup chopped onion
1	can (10-3/4 ounces) condensed cream of mushroom soup, undiluted
1/2	pound fresh mushrooms, chopped
1/2	teaspoon onion salt
1/2	teaspoon seasoned salt
1/8	teaspoon pepper
4	cups (16 ounces) shredded part-skim mozzarella cheese

Optional toppings: sour cream, jalapeno peppers, hot pepper sauce

In a mixing bowl, dissolve yeast in water. Add oil, salt, sugar and 2 cups flour; beat until smooth. Add enough remaining flour to form a soft dough.

Turn onto a floured surface; knead until smooth and elastic, about 6-8 minutes. Place in a greased bowl, turning once to grease top. Cover and let rise in a warm place until doubled, about 1 hour.

Meanwhile, in a skillet, cook beef and onion over medium heat until meat is no longer pink; drain. Add soup, mushrooms and seasonings; set aside.

Punch dough down; divide in half. On a floured surface, roll each portion of dough into a 15-in. x 10-in. rectangle. Transfer to a greased baking sheet.

Spoon the beef mixture lengthwise down half of the rectangle to within 1 in. of edges. Fold dough over filling. Pinch edges to seal. Cut four diagonal slits on top of loaves. Cover and let rise until doubled, about 45 minutes.

Bake at 350° for 30-35 minutes or until golden brown. Cut into slices. Serve warm with toppings of your choice. YIELD: 2 LOAVES.

EDITOR'S NOTE: When cutting hot peppers, disposable gloves are recommended. Avoid touching your face.

Savory Herb Cheesecake

LEE-ANNE HAMILTON • LOUISBURG, KANSAS

I came across the recipe for this pleasing appetizer while taking an herb gardening course. It was the hit of the buffet at our "End of Class" party.

PREP: 15 min. **COOK:** 35 min. + chilling

3	packages (8 ounces *each*) reduced-fat cream cheese, cubed
2	cups (16 ounces) reduced-fat sour cream, *divided*
1	can (10-3/4 ounces) reduced-fat condensed cream of broccoli soup, undiluted
3/4	cup egg substitute
1/2	cup grated Romano cheese
2	to 4 tablespoons minced fresh basil
1	to 2 tablespoons minced fresh thyme
1	tablespoon cornstarch
1	to 2 teaspoons minced fresh tarragon
2	garlic cloves, minced
1/2	teaspoon coarsely ground pepper
3	tablespoons *each* chopped sweet red, yellow and orange pepper
3	tablespoons minced chives

Assorted crackers *or* fresh vegetables

In a large mixing bowl, combine the cream cheese, 1 cup sour cream and soup; beat until smooth. Add egg substitute; beat on low just until combined. Add the Romano cheese, basil, thyme, cornstarch, tarragon, garlic and pepper; beat just until blended.

Pour into a 9-in. springform pan coated with cooking spray. Place pan on a baking sheet. Bake at 350° for 35-45 minutes or until center is almost set. Turn oven off; leave cheesecake in oven with door ajar for 30 minutes.

Remove from oven. Carefully run a knife around the edge of pan to loosen. Cool for 1 hour longer. Refrigerate overnight. Remove sides of pan. Just before serving, spread with remaining sour cream. Garnish with chopped peppers and chives. Serve with crackers or fresh vegetables. YIELD: 24 SERVINGS.

savory herb cheesecake

Poppy Seed Squares

JO BADEN • INDEPENDENCE, KANSAS

When I found this delightfully different appetizer, I just knew I had to try it. Although I prepare these squares every Christmas, no one tires of them.

PREP: 35 min. **BAKE:** 25 min.

1	pound ground beef
1-1/2	cups finely chopped fresh mushrooms
1	medium onion, finely chopped
1	can (10-3/4 ounces) condensed cream of celery soup, *or* mushroom soup, undiluted
1	tablespoon prepared horseradish
1	teaspoon salt
1/2	teaspoon pepper

CRUST:

3	cups all-purpose flour
2	tablespoons poppy seeds
3/4	teaspoon baking powder
3/4	teaspoon salt
1	cup shortening
1/2	cup cold water

In a skillet, cook beef, mushrooms and onion over medium heat until meat is no longer pink. Add the soup, horseradish, salt and pepper; mix well. Remove from the heat; set aside.

In a bowl, combine the flour, poppy seeds, baking powder and salt. Cut in shortening until the mixture resembles coarse crumbs. Gradually add water, tossing with a fork until a ball forms. Divide dough in half. Roll out one portion into a 15-in. x 10-in. rectangle; transfer to an ungreased 15-in. x 10-in. x 1-in. baking pan.

poppy seed squares

Spoon the meat mixture over the dough. Roll out the remaining dough into 15-in. x 10-in rectangle; place over filling. Bake at 425° for 25 minutes or until golden brown. Cut into small appetizer squares. YIELD: ABOUT 10 DOZEN.

Hot 'n' Cheesy Chicken Sandwiches

NANCY FREDERIKSEN • SPRINGFIELD, MINNESOTA

This is a great sandwich when you need to feed a crowd. It takes only minutes to assemble before being baked in the oven.

PREP: 10 min. **BAKE:** 45 min.

6	cups cubed cooked chicken
1-1/2	cups chopped celery
1	can (10-3/4 ounces) condensed cream of mushroom soup, undiluted
3/4	cup mayonnaise
3/4	cup chopped green pepper
1	teaspoon ground mustard
1/2	teaspoon salt
1/2	teaspoon pepper
3	cups process cheese (Velveeta), cubed
24	hamburger buns, split

In a large bowl, combine the first eight ingredients. Pour mixture into an ungreased 2-1/2-qt. casserole; top with cheese.

Cover and bake at 350° for 45 minutes or until bubbly. Let stand for 5 minutes; spoon 1/3 cup onto each bun. YIELD: 24 SERVINGS.

Mushroom Burger Cups

LUCILLE METCALFE • BARRIE, ONTARIO

For many years on Christmas Eve, my friend would bring these hearty snacks to share with our six children and us. Now our grandchildren nibble on these treats as the adults reminisce about past holidays.

PREP: 25 min. **BAKE:** 35 min.

18	slices bread, crusts removed
1/4	cup butter, softened
1	pound ground beef, cooked and drained
1	can (10-3/4 ounces) condensed cream of mushroom soup, undiluted
1	egg, beaten

1/2 cup shredded cheddar cheese
1/4 cup chopped onion
1 teaspoon Worcestershire sauce
Salt and pepper to taste

Using a biscuit cutter, cut 2-1/2-in. circles from bread slices. Spread butter over one side of each circle. Press circles, buttered side down, into ungreased miniature muffin cups.

In a bowl, combine the remaining ingredients; mix well. Spoon into bread cups. Bake at 350° for 35 minutes or until golden brown. YIELD: 1-1/2 DOZEN.

EDITOR'S NOTE: You can keep a batch of Mushroom Burger Cups on hand for easy entertaining. After baking them, cool, then freeze in an airtight container for up to 3 months. Reheat frozen cups on a baking sheet at 350° for 20 minutes or until heated through.

Make-Ahead Saucy Sandwiches

ELIZABETH ROTHERT • KERNVILLE, CALIFORNIA

I've made these sandwiches many times for luncheons and light dinners. They can be prepared ahead of time and popped in the oven when needed.

PREP: 15 min. + freezing **BAKE:** 50 min.

24 slices white sandwich bread
1-1/2 cups diced cooked chicken
1 can (10-3/4 ounces) condensed cream of mushroom soup, undiluted
1/2 cup prepared chicken gravy
1 can (8 ounces) water chestnuts, drained and chopped
1 jar (2 ounces) chopped pimientos, drained
2 tablespoons chopped green onions
Salt and pepper to taste
5 eggs
1/3 cup milk
2 bags (6 ounces *each*) ridged potato chips, crushed

Trim crusts from bread. (Discard or save for another use.) In a medium bowl, combine chicken, soup, gravy, water chestnuts, pimientos, onions, salt and pepper. Spread on 12 slices of bread; top with remaining bread. Wrap each in foil and freeze.

In a bowl, beat eggs and milk. Unwrap sandwiches; dip frozen sandwiches in egg mixture and then in potato chips.

Place sandwiches on greased baking sheets. Bake at 325° for 50-60 minutes or until golden brown. YIELD: 12 SERVINGS.

chicken enchilada dip

Chicken Enchilada Dip

LEAH DAVIS • MORROW, OHIO

A friend brought this cheesy dip to our house for a dinner party. Everyone loved the zesty chicken and southwestern flavor so much that no one was hungry for supper. My friend graciously shared the recipe, and I've served it many times, always with rave reviews.

PREP/TOTAL TIME: 20 min.

2 cups shredded cooked chicken
1 can (10-3/4 ounces) condensed cream of chicken soup, undiluted
1 cup (4 ounces) shredded cheddar cheese
1 can (5 ounces) evaporated milk
1/2 cup chopped celery
1/3 cup finely chopped onion
1 can (4 ounces) chopped green chilies
1 envelope taco seasoning
Tortilla chips

In a 2-qt. microwave-safe dish, combine the first eight ingredients. Microwave, uncovered, on high for 4-5 minutes; stir. Microwave, uncovered, 3-4 minutes longer or until heated through. Serve with tortilla chips. YIELD: 3 CUPS.

EDITOR'S NOTE: This recipe was tested in a 1,100-watt microwave.

crab cheese fondue

Crab Cheese Fondue

MARY HOUCHIN • SWANSEA, ILLINOIS

We used to host fondue parties regularly with our friends and tried to outdo each other with the most wonderful recipes. This thick and cheesy blend with its mild crab flavor was always a hit.

PREP/TOTAL TIME: 15 min.

3/4	cup milk
1/2	cup condensed cream of mushroom *or* celery soup, undiluted
2	cups (8 ounces) shredded cheddar cheese
8	ounces process cheese (Velveeta), cubed
1	can (6 ounces) crabmeat, drained, flaked and cartilage removed
2	teaspoons lemon juice
1	garlic clove, halved

Cubed French bread, cherry tomatoes, baby zucchini, cooked new potatoes *and/or* artichoke hearts for dipping

In a saucepan, combine milk and soup until blended. Add cheeses; cook and stir over low heat until melted. Stir in the crab and lemon juice; remove from the heat.

Rub the interior of a fondue pot with the cut side of garlic; discard garlic. Pour cheese mixture into pot; keep at a gentle simmer over low heat. Serve with bread cubes, tomatoes, zucchini, potatoes and/or artichoke hearts. YIELD: 3 CUPS.

Spinach Feta Squares

CHRISTINE HALANDRAS • MEEKER, COLORADO

"A real crowd-pleaser" is how I describe this baked spinach appetizer. I love that you can make it ahead of time to reheat later or serve cold. The yummy squares even make a delicious vegetable entree or side dish—just cut the pieces a little larger.

PREP: 10 min. **BAKE:** 45 min.

1	large onion, chopped
3	tablespoons butter
2	packages (10 ounces *each*) frozen chopped spinach, thawed and squeezed dry
1	can (10-3/4 ounces) condensed cream of mushroom soup, undiluted
4	eggs, beaten
1	cup sliced fresh mushrooms
1/4	cup dried bread crumbs
1/4	cup crumbled feta *or* blue cheese
1/8	teaspoon dried oregano
1/8	teaspoon dried basil

Dash ground nutmeg

Salt and pepper to taste

2	tablespoons grated Parmesan cheese

In a skillet, saute onion in butter. Add spinach, soup, eggs, mushrooms, bread crumbs, feta cheese, oregano, basil, nutmeg, salt and pepper. Spoon into a greased 9-in. square baking pan. Sprinkle with Parmesan cheese.

Bake, uncovered, at 325° for 45-50 minutes or until a knife inserted near the center comes out clean. Cut into 1-in. squares. YIELD: ABOUT 6-1/2 DOZEN.

cooking tip

When a recipe calls for grated Parmesan cheese, it makes no difference whether you grate your own or buy already grated cheese at the store. If you decide to buy a chunk of Parmesan cheese and grate your own, be sure to use the finest section on your grating tool.

herbed cheesecake

Herbed Cheesecake

JULIE TOMLIN • WATKINSVILLE, GEORGIA

Cheesecake isn't just for dessert! This savory version served with crackers is a favorite starter that keeps dozens of party guests happily munching.

PREP: 15 min. **BAKE:** 55 min. + chilling

3	packages (8 ounces *each*) cream cheese, softened
2	cups (16 ounces) sour cream, *divided*
1	can (10-3/4 ounces) condensed cream of celery soup, undiluted
3	eggs
1/2	cup grated Romano cheese
3	garlic cloves, minced
1	tablespoon cornstarch
2	tablespoons minced fresh basil *or* 2 teaspoons dried basil
1	tablespoon minced fresh thyme *or* 1 teaspoon dried thyme
1/2	teaspoon Italian seasoning
1/2	teaspoon coarsely ground pepper

Assorted crackers

In a large mixing bowl, beat the cream cheese, 1 cup sour cream and soup until smooth. Add the eggs, Romano cheese, garlic, cornstarch, basil, thyme, Italian seasoning and pepper; beat until smooth.

Pour into a greased 9-in. springform pan. Place pan on a baking sheet. Bake at 350° for 55-60 minutes or until center is almost set. Cool on a wire rack for 10 minutes. Carefully run a knife around edge of pan to loosen; cool 1 hour longer.

Refrigerate for at least 4 hours or overnight. Remove sides of pan. Spread remaining sour cream over top. Serve with crackers. Refrigerate leftovers. YIELD: 24 SERVINGS.

Turkey Crescents

MARYE JO TIMMONS • ALEXANDRIA, VIRGINIA

Refrigerated crescent rolls and mushroom soup make the golden bites simple, while a filling of turkey, onion and celery makes them delicious.

PREP/TOTAL TIME: 30 min.

1/2	cup finely chopped celery
1/4	cup finely chopped onion
1	teaspoon butter
2	cups finely chopped cooked turkey
1	can (10-3/4 ounces) condensed cream of mushroom soup, undiluted
3	packages (8 ounces *each*) refrigerated crescent rolls

Dill weed

In a nonstick skillet, saute celery and onion in butter for 3-4 minutes or until tender. Add turkey and soup; mix well. Remove from the heat.

Separate crescent roll dough into 24 triangles. Place 1 tablespoon turkey mixture on the wide end of each triangle; roll up from wide end. Place pointed side down 2 in. apart on greased baking sheets. Curve ends to form crescent shape. Sprinkle the crescents with dill.

Bake at 350° for 8-9 minutes or until golden brown. Serve immediately. YIELD: 2 DOZEN.

turkey crescents

Warm Broccoli Cheese Dip

BARBARA MAIOL • CONYERS, GEORGIA

When my family gets together, this flavorful, creamy dip is always served. Everyone loves its zip from the jalapeno pepper and its crunch from the broccoli.

PREP: 15 min. **COOK:** 2-1/2 hours

2	jars (8 ounces *each*) process cheese sauce
1	can (10-3/4 ounces) condensed cream of chicken soup, undiluted
3	cups frozen chopped broccoli, thawed and drained
1/2	pound fresh mushrooms, chopped
2	tablespoons chopped seeded jalapeno pepper

Assorted fresh vegetables

In a 1-1/2-qt. slow cooker, combine the cheese sauce and soup. Cover and cook on low for 30 minutes or until cheese is melted, stirring occasionally.

Stir in the broccoli, mushrooms and jalapeno. Cover and cook on low for 2 hours or until heated through. Serve dip with assorted fresh vegetables. YIELD: 5-1/2 CUPS.

EDITOR'S NOTE: When cutting hot peppers, disposable gloves are recommended. Avoid touching your face.

warm broccoli cheese dip

Three-Two-One Dip

EVELYN SHAULIS • BUTLER, PENNSYLVANIA

During my husband's teaching career, we did a lot of entertaining. I'd throw together this rich dip in just minutes, and it always received praise.

PREP/TOTAL TIME: 15 min.

3	packages (8 ounces *each*) cream cheese, cubed
2	cans (10-3/4 ounces *each*) condensed cream of celery soup, undiluted
1	pound sliced pepperoni, finely chopped

Assorted crackers

In a large saucepan, combine the cream cheese, soup and pepperoni. Cook and stir over medium-low heat until cheese is melted. Serve warm with crackers. YIELD: 6 CUPS.

Beef-Stuffed French Bread

ERIN GEE • FORT COLLINS, COLORADO

A wonderful lady in Spanish Fork, Utah shared this recipe with me—it fed her large farm family, and now I serve it to my family and friends. Using Colorado beef and an Idaho potato makes this hearty sandwich a real Western meal! If you have a leftover baked potato from dinner, this is a perfect way to use it.

PREP: 25 min. **BAKE:** 20 min. + chilling

1	pound ground beef
1/2	cup chopped onion
1	large baked potato, peeled and cubed
1	can (10-3/4 ounces) condensed cream of mushroom soup, undiluted
1	can (4 ounces) mushroom stems and pieces, drained
1	teaspoon dried parsley flakes
1/4	teaspoon garlic powder
1/8	teaspoon pepper

Dash hot pepper sauce

1	loaf (1 pound) French bread
1	cup (4 ounces) shredded cheddar cheese

In a large skillet, cook the beef and onion over medium heat until meat is no longer pink; drain. Add the potato, soup, mushrooms, parsley, garlic powder, pepper and hot pepper sauce; cover and simmer for 10 minutes.

Meanwhile, cut the loaf of bread in half lengthwise. Hollow out bottom of loaf, leaving a 3/4-in. shell; set aside. Place the removed bread in a blender; cover and process until crumbled. Add 1 cup of crumbs to beef mixture (save remaining crumbs for another use). Stir in cheese.

Spoon beef mixture into bread shell; replace bread top. Wrap in heavy-duty foil; place on a baking sheet. Bake at 30° for 20 minutes. Let stand for 5 minutes before slicing. YIELD: 6-8 SERVINGS.

Slow-Cooked Turkey Sandwiches

DIANE TWAIT NELSEN • RINGSTED, IOWA

These slow-cooked sandwiches have been such a hit at office potlucks that I keep copies of the recipe in my desk to hand out to my co-workers.

PREP: 15 min. **COOK:** 3 hours

6	cups cubed cooked turkey
2	cups cubed process cheese (Velveeta)
1	can (10-3/4 ounces) condensed cream of chicken soup, undiluted
1	can (10-3/4 ounces) condensed cream of mushroom soup, undiluted
1/2	cup finely chopped onion
1/2	cup chopped celery
22	wheat sandwich buns, split

In a 3-qt. slow cooker, combine the first six ingredients. Cover and cook on low for 3-4 hours or until onion and celery are tender and cheese is melted. Stir before spooning onto buns. YIELD: 22 SERVINGS.

cooking tip

For picture-perfect presentation of any molded appetizer, try either of these simple tricks. Before inverting the mold onto a platter, place it up to its rim in a large pan of warm water until the edges begin to pull away from sides. Or, turn the chilled mold over a serving platter and drape a damp, hot towel over the top for a few minutes.

Molded Shrimp Spread

MRS. AUSTIN LOCKE • PRINEVILLE, OREGON

I usually make this savory cracker spread for parties and family gatherings. It never lasts very long on the buffet because folks go straight for it.

PREP: 15 min. + chilling

1	can (10-3/4 ounces) condensed cream of mushroom soup, undiluted
1	package (8 ounces) cream cheese, cubed
1	envelope unflavored gelatin
3	tablespoons cold water
1	cup finely chopped celery
1	cup mayonnaise
3	tablespoons lemon juice
4	green onions, finely chopped
1/2	pound cooked shrimp, peeled, deveined and coarsely chopped

Lettuce leaves and additional shrimp, optional
Assorted crackers

In a saucepan, heat soup and cream cheese over medium heat until cheese is melted, stirring frequently. Remove from the heat; set aside to cool.

In a small microwave-safe bowl, sprinkle gelatin over water; let stand for 1 minute. Microwave on high for 40 seconds; stir. Let stand for 2 minutes or until gelatin is completely dissolved. Stir the gelatin mixture, celery, mayonnaise, lemon juice and onions into soup mixture. Fold in shrimp.

Pour into a 5-cup ring mold coated with cooking spray. Cover and refrigerate for 8 hours or until set. Invert onto a serving plate. Fill center of ring with lettuce and shrimp if desired. Serve with crackers. YIELD: 4-1/4 CUPS.

CHAPTER 2
Soups

Meatball Mushroom Soup

JOANN ABBOTT • KERHONKSON, NEW YORK

This creamy, super-thick soup is hearty with meatballs, mushrooms, barley, macaroni and rice. With dinner rolls or breadsticks, it's a simple and satisfying meal for my husband and me on a rainy day. Leftovers easily reheat for a fast, filling lunch or dinner.

PREP/TOTAL TIME: 30 min.

1/2	pound ground beef
2	cans (10-3/4 ounces *each*) condensed cream of mushroom soup, undiluted
1-1/3	cups milk
1-1/3	cups water
1	teaspoon Italian seasoning
1	teaspoon dried minced onion
1/2	teaspoon dried minced garlic
1/4	cup quick-cooking barley
1/4	cup uncooked elbow macaroni
1/4	cup uncooked long grain rice
1	medium carrot, shredded
1	jar (4-1/2 ounces) sliced mushrooms, drained
2	tablespoons grated Parmesan cheese

Shape beef into 1-in. balls; set aside. In a large saucepan, combine soup, milk and water; bring to a boil. Add Italian seasoning, onion, garlic, barley, macaroni and rice. Reduce heat; simmer, uncovered, for 15 minutes.

Meanwhile, brown meatballs in a nonstick skillet until no longer pink. Stir carrot into soup; cover and simmer for 5 minutes. Use a slotted spoon to transfer meatballs to soup. Stir in mushrooms and Parmesan cheese; heat through. YIELD: 6 SERVINGS.

cooking tip

If you want to make that creamy soup even thicker, here's an easy and inexpensive way. Reach for a box of mashed potato flakes. Stir the flakes into the simmering soup a little at a time until you reach the desired consistency.

halibut chowder

Halibut Chowder

MARY DAVIS • PALMER, ALASKA

This rich, comforting chowder is so good you won't believe it starts with canned soup and frozen vegetables. It showcases tender chunks of halibut, but salmon or most any type of whitefish will do. I double the recipe for large gatherings...each time I serve it, my guests practically lick the pot clean.

PREP/TOTAL TIME: 20 min.

8	to 10 green onions, thinly sliced
2	garlic cloves, minced
2	tablespoons butter
4	cans (10-3/4 ounces *each*) condensed cream of potato soup, undiluted
2	cans (10-3/4 ounces *each*) condensed cream of mushroom soup, undiluted
4	cups milk
2	packages (8 ounces *each*) cream cheese, cubed
1-1/2	pounds halibut *or* salmon fillets, cubed
1-1/2	cups frozen sliced carrots
1-1/2	cups frozen corn
1/8	to 1/4 teaspoon cayenne pepper, optional

In a Dutch oven or soup kettle, saute onions and garlic in butter until tender. Add soups, milk and cream cheese; cook and stir until cheese is melted. Bring to a boil.

Stir in fish, carrots and corn. Reduce heat; simmer, uncovered, for 5-10 minutes or until fish flakes easily and the vegetables are tender. Add cayenne pepper if desired. YIELD: 16 SERVINGS (ABOUT 4 QUARTS).

lemony turkey rice soup

Lemony Turkey Rice Soup

MARGARITA CUELLAR • EAST CHICAGO, INDIANA

While growing up in Texas, I spent a lot of time help-ing my grandma cook. Lemon juice and cilantro add a deliciously different twist to turkey soup.

PREP/TOTAL TIME: 20 min.

6	cups chicken broth, *divided*
1	can (10-3/4 ounces) condensed cream of chicken soup, undiluted
2	cups cooked rice
2	cups diced cooked turkey
1/4	teaspoon pepper
2	tablespoons cornstarch
1/4	to 1/3 cup lemon juice
1/4	to 1/2 cup minced fresh cilantro

In a large saucepan, combine 5-1/2 cups of broth, soup, rice, turkey and pepper. Bring to a boil; boil for 3 minutes. In a small bowl, combine cornstarch and remaining broth until smooth. Gradually stir in-to hot soup. Cook and stir for 1-2 minutes or until thickened and heated through. Remove from the heat; stir in lemon juice and cilantro. YIELD: 8 SERVINGS (ABOUT 2 QUARTS).

Potato Clam Chowder

KRISTY DOTY • RIVERSIDE, CALIFORNIA

This recipe comes from an old college friend. Pair steam-ing bowlfuls with sourdough bread and a green salad.

PREP/TOTAL TIME: 30 min.

1/2	pound sliced bacon, diced
2	large onions, chopped
3	cans (6-1/2 ounces *each*) minced clams
3	cups diced unpeeled potatoes
1/2	cup chicken broth
1	can (10-3/4 ounces) condensed cream of celery soup, undiluted
1-1/4	cups milk
1	cup heavy whipping cream
1	teaspoon salt
1/2	teaspoon pepper

In a Dutch oven or soup kettle, cook bacon over medium heat until crisp. Using a slotted spoon, re-move to paper towels; drain, reserving 2 tablespoons drippings. In the drippings, saute onions until tender. Drain clams, reserving juice. Set clams aside. Add the potatoes, clam juice and broth to the onions. Cook over medium heat for 15 minutes or until potatoes are tender. Stir in the clams, soup, milk, cream, salt, pepper and bacon; heat through. YIELD: 8 SERVINGS (2 QUARTS).

Super-Duper Chili

ELIZABETH MAYS • NUNNELLY, TENNESSEE

No one ever guesses the "secret ingredient" in this recipe that I created—a can of cream of mushroom soup! It makes the chili so thick and creamy. Take this spicy concoction to a fall potluck or church dinner, and watch folks warm up to it!

PREP: 20 min. **COOK:** 30 min.

1	pound bulk pork sausage
1	pound ground beef
2	cans (15-1/2 ounces *each*) hot chili beans
1	jar (16 ounces) salsa
1	can (16 ounces) kidney beans, rinsed and drained
1	can (15 ounces) pinto beans, rinsed and drained
1	can (14-1/2 ounces) diced tomatoes, undrained
1	can (10-3/4 ounces) condensed cream of mushroom soup, undiluted
1	can (8 ounces) tomato sauce
8	ounces process cheese (Velveeta), cubed
1-1/2	teaspoons chili powder
1/2	teaspoon cayenne pepper

In a large soup kettle or Dutch oven, cook the sausage and beef over medium heat until no longer pink; drain. Stir in the remaining ingredients. Bring to a boil. Reduce heat; cover and simmer for 30 min-utes or until chili is heated through. YIELD: 14 SERVINGS (3-1/2 QUARTS).

Tuscan Turkey Sausage Soup

THOMAS LICKING • GREEN LAKE, WISCONSIN

While trying to reproduce my favorite soup from an Italian restaurant's menu, I hit upon this tasty combination of turkey sausage, broth and mushrooms. Fennel, caraway seeds and herb seasoning give the quick-to-fix soup plenty of flavor without adding salt.

PREP/TOTAL TIME: 30 min.

- 12 ounces turkey Italian sausage links
- 4 cups reduced-sodium chicken broth
- 1 can (10-3/4 ounces) reduced-fat reduced-sodium condensed cream of chicken soup, undiluted
- 1 can (8 ounces) mushroom stems and pieces, drained
- 1 small onion, chopped
- 1 tablespoon Italian seasoning
- 1/4 teaspoon salt-free garlic and herb seasoning
- 1/8 teaspoon caraway seeds
- 1/8 teaspoon fennel seed, crushed
- 1 can (15-1/2 ounces) great northern beans, rinsed and drained
- 1 small leek (white potion only), cut into 1-inch strips

In a nonstick skillet coated with cooking spray, cook sausage over medium heat until no longer pink; drain. Let cool and slice.

In a large saucepan, whisk together the broth, soup, mushrooms, onion, Italian seasoning, garlic and herb seasoning, caraway seeds and fennel seed. Add sausage. Bring to a boil.

Reduce heat; simmer, uncovered, for 5 minutes. Add beans and leek. Simmer 10 minutes longer or until vegetables are tender. YIELD: 8 SERVINGS.

Rosemary Mushroom Soup

SANDRA BURROWS • COVENTRY, CONNECTICUT

The inviting, piney fragrance and flavor of rosemary really adds spark to this tasty mushroom soup. I hope you enjoy it as much as I do!

PREP/TOTAL TIME: 15 min.

- 1 cup sliced fresh mushrooms
- 2 garlic cloves, minced
- 1/4 cup butter

- 1 can (10-3/4 ounces) condensed cream of mushroom soup, undiluted
- 1 cup half-and-half cream
- 1 tablespoon minced fresh rosemary *or* 1 teaspoon dried rosemary, crushed
- 1/2 teaspoon paprika
- 2 tablespoons minced chives

In a large saucepan, saute mushrooms and garlic in butter until tender. Stir in soup, cream, rosemary and paprika; heat through but do not boil. Sprinkle with chives. YIELD: 3 SERVINGS.

Tomato Hamburger Soup

JULIE KRUGER • ST. CLOUD, MINNESOTA

As a full-time teacher, I only have time to cook from scratch a few nights each week. This recipe makes a big enough batch to feed my family for two nights.

PREP: 5 min. **COOK:** 4 hours

- 1 can (46 ounces) V8 juice
- 2 packages (16 ounces *each*) frozen mixed vegetables
- 1 pound ground beef, cooked and drained
- 1 can (10-3/4 ounces) condensed cream of mushroom soup, undiluted
- 2 teaspoons dried minced onion
Salt and pepper to taste

In a 5-qt. slow cooker, combine the first five ingredients; mix well. Cover and cook on high for 4 hours or until heated through. Season with salt and pepper. YIELD: 12 SERVINGS (3 QUARTS).

tomato hamburger soup

Chunky Chicken Soup

NANCY CLOW • MALLORYTOWN, ONTARIO

I am a stay-at-home mom who relies on my slow cooker for fast, nutritious meals that have minimal cleanup and prep time. I knew this recipe was a real winner when I did not have any leftovers and my husband asked me to make the soup again.

PREP: 15 min. **COOK:** 4-1/2 hours

1-1/2	pounds boneless skinless chicken breasts, cut into 2-inch strips
2	teaspoons vegetable oil
2/3	cup finely chopped onion
2	medium carrots, chopped
2	celery ribs, chopped
1	cup frozen corn
2	cans (10-3/4 ounces *each*) condensed cream of potato soup, undiluted
1-1/2	cups chicken broth
1	teaspoon dill weed
1	cup frozen peas
1/2	cup half-and-half cream

In a large skillet over medium-high heat, brown chicken in vegetable oil. With a slotted spoon, transfer chicken to a 5-qt. slow cooker. Add the onion, carrots, celery and corn. In a small bowl, whisk the soup, broth and dill until blended; stir into slow cooker.

Cover and cook on low for 4 hours or until the vegetables are tender. Stir in peas and cream. Cover and cook 30 minutes longer or until heated through. YIELD: 7 SERVINGS.

chunky chicken soup

Italian Meatball Soup

SUE FULLER • QUINCY, MICHIGAN

After a busy day of running errands and cleaning, I wanted something quick but hearty for dinner. To do that, I combined prepared meatballs with canned soup, mushrooms and seasonings. My husband loved my creation and thought I spent hours preparing it.

PREP/TOTAL TIME: 10 min.

2	cans (10-3/4 ounces *each*) condensed cream of mushroom soup, undiluted
2-2/3	cups milk
1/2	teaspoon dried oregano
1/8	to 1/4 teaspoon pepper
24	frozen cooked Italian meatballs (1/2 ounce *each*), thawed
1	jar (4-1/2 ounces) sliced mushrooms, drained

In a large saucepan, whisk the soup, milk, oregano and pepper until blended. Add the meat balls and mushrooms. Cover and cook until heated through. YIELD: 6 SERVINGS.

Beefy Wild Rice Soup

MARILYN CHESBROUGH • WAUTOMA, WISCONSIN

Living in central Wisconsin, we experience many days of snow and cold temperatures. I like to prepare soup often, especially this one. My family loves it.

PREP: 15 min. **COOK:** 1 hour 15 min.

1	pound ground beef
1/2	teaspoon Italian seasoning
6	cups water, *divided*
2	large onions, chopped
3	celery ribs, chopped
1	cup uncooked wild rice
2	teaspoons beef bouillon granules
1/2	teaspoon pepper
1/4	teaspoon hot pepper sauce
3	cans (10-3/4 ounces *each*) condensed cream of mushroom soup, undiluted
1	can (4 ounces) mushroom stems and pieces, drained

In a Dutch oven or soup kettle, cook beef and Italian seasoning over medium heat until meat is no longer pink; drain. Add 2 cups water, onions, celery, rice, bouillon, pepper and hot pepper sauce; bring to a boil.

Reduce heat; cover and simmer for 45 minutes. Stir in the soup, mushrooms and remaining water. Cover and simmer soup for 30 minutes. YIELD: 10-12 SERVINGS (3 QUARTS).

Harvest Corn Chowder

CAROLYN LOUGH • MEDLEY, ALBERTA

Perfect for those cooler autumn days, this chowder features a bounty of harvest flavors. Corn, potatoes, mushrooms and peppers come together beautifully— especially since several of the ingredients call for convenient canned items.

PREP/TOTAL TIME: 20 min.

1	medium onion, chopped
1	tablespoon butter
2	cans (14-1/2 ounces *each*) cream-style corn
4	cups whole kernel corn
4	cups diced peeled potatoes
1	can (10-3/4 ounces) condensed cream of mushroom soup, undiluted
1	jar (6 ounces) sliced mushrooms, drained
3	cups milk
1/2	medium green pepper, chopped
1/2	to 1 medium sweet red pepper, chopped
Pepper to taste	
1/2	pound bacon, cooked and crumbled

In a saucepan, saute onion in butter until tender. Add cream-style corn, kernel corn, potatoes, soup and mushrooms. Stir in milk. Add green and red peppers. Season with pepper. Simmer for 30 minutes or until vegetables are tender. Garnish with bacon. YIELD: ABOUT 12 SERVINGS (3-1/2 QUARTS).

cooking tip

Looking for a speedy way to chop onions without tears? Consider your blender. Quarter the onions, place them in a blender and cover with water. Put the top back on the blender and process on high speed for a second or two until chopped. Drain the onions and you're done!

slow-cooked corn chowder

Slow-Cooked Corn Chowder

MARY HOGUE • ROCHESTER, PENNSYLVANIA

I combine and refrigerate the ingredients for this easy chowder the night before. In the morning, I simply pour the mixture into the slow cooker and turn it on before I leave for work. When I come home in the evening, a hot, home-cooked meal awaits.

PREP: 10 min. **COOK:** 6 hours

2-1/2	cups milk
1	can (14-3/4 ounces) cream-style corn
1	can (10-3/4 ounces) condensed cream of mushroom soup, undiluted
1-3/4	cups frozen corn
1	cup frozen shredded hash brown potatoes
1	cup cubed fully cooked ham
1	large onion, chopped
2	teaspoons dried parsley flakes
2	tablespoons butter
Salt and pepper to taste	

In a 3-qt. slow cooker, combine all of the ingredients. Cover and cook chowder on low for 6 hours. YIELD: 8 SERVINGS (2 QUARTS).

shrimp chowder

Cover and cook on low for 3 hours. Stir in shrimp and cream cheese. Cook 30 minutes longer or until shrimp are heated through and cheese is melted. Stir to blend. YIELD: 12 SERVINGS (3 QUARTS).

EDITOR'S NOTE: The following spices may be substituted for 1 teaspoon Creole seasoning: 1/4 teaspoon *each* salt, garlic powder and paprika; and a pinch *each* of dried thyme, ground cumin and cayenne pepper.

Country Carrot Soup

MARLANE JONES • ALLENTOWN, PENNSYLVANIA

I used ground beef to jazz up a traditional carrot soup recipe. This meaty meal-in-a-bowl always hits the spot. Serve it with freshly baked bread.

PREP/TOTAL TIME: 30 min.

1	pound ground beef
1/4	cup chopped onion
2	cans (10-3/4 ounces *each*) condensed cream of celery soup, undiluted
3	cups tomato juice
2	cups shredded carrots
1	cup water
1	bay leaf
1/2	teaspoon sugar
1/2	teaspoon dried marjoram
1/2	teaspoon salt
1/4	teaspoon garlic powder
1/4	teaspoon pepper

In a large saucepan, brown beef and onion over medium heat until beef is no longer pink; drain. Add remaining ingredients; bring to a boil. Reduce heat; cover and simmer for 15 minutes or until carrots are tender. Remove bay leaf. YIELD: 6-8 SERVINGS.

Zesty Cheeseburger Soup

NORMA ROWE • WINFIELD, KANSAS

A dear friend shared this recipe with me. Every time I serve it, I'm met with recipe requests. Even my son-in-law, who's a picky eater, can't get enough of this soup!

PREP: 10 min. **COOK:** 35 min.

2	pounds ground beef
1	medium onion, chopped
Salt, pepper and garlic powder to taste	
1-1/2	cups cubed peeled potatoes

Shrimp Chowder

WILL ZUNIO • GRETNA, LOUISIANA

This rich and creamy creation simmers in my slow cooker for a delicious meal. Because the chowder is ready in less than four hours, it can be prepared in the afternoon and served that night.

PREP: 15 min. **BAKE:** 3-1/2 hours

1/2	cup chopped onion
2	teaspoons butter
2	cans (12 ounces *each*) evaporated milk
2	cans (10-3/4 ounces *each*) condensed cream of potato soup, undiluted
2	cans (10-3/4 ounces *each*) condensed cream of chicken soup, undiluted
1	can (11 ounces) white *or* shoepeg corn, drained
1	teaspoon Creole seasoning
1/2	teaspoon garlic powder
2	pounds cooked small shrimp, peeled and deveined
1	package (3 ounces) cream cheese, cubed

In a small skillet, saute onion in butter until tender. In a 5-qt. slow cooker, combine the onion, milk, soups, corn, Creole seasoning and garlic powder.

1-1/2 cups water
1 can (15-1/4 ounces) whole kernel corn, drained
1 can (14-3/4 ounces) cream-style corn
1 can (11 ounces) condensed cheddar cheese soup, undiluted
1 can (10-3/4 ounces) condensed cream of asparagus soup, undiluted
1 can (10-3/4 ounces) condensed cream of mushroom soup, undiluted
1 can (10 ounces) diced tomatoes and green chilies
2 cups half-and-half cream

In a soup kettle or Dutch oven, cook beef, onion, salt, pepper and garlic powder over medium heat until meat is no longer pink; drain.

Add potatoes and water; bring to a boil. Reduce heat; cover and simmer for 15-20 minutes or until the potatoes are tender. Add the corn, soups and tomatoes; mix well. Bring to a boil. Reduce heat. Stir in cream; heat through but do not boil. YIELD: 14-16 SERVINGS (3-3/4 QUARTS).

Reuben Chowder

IOLA EGLE • BELLA VISTA, ARKANSAS

If you like Reuben sandwiches, you'll be delighted with the flavor of this soup. Crunchy rye bread croutons top a hearty blend of convenient canned soups, sauerkraut, corned beef and mozzarella cheese. I like to make it a meal by adding a green salad and a basket of warm rolls.

PREP/TOTAL TIME: 30 min.

1 tablespoon butter
3 slices rye bread
1 can (11 ounces) condensed nacho cheese soup, undiluted
1 can (10-3/4 ounces) condensed cream of mushroom soup, undiluted
3 cups milk
1 can (14 ounces) sauerkraut, rinsed and drained
12 ounces deli corned beef, diced
1 cup (4 ounces) shredded part-skim mozzarella cheese

Butter bread on both sides; cube. Place bread on an ungreased baking sheet. Bake at 375° for 6-8 minutes or until browned.

Meanwhile, in a large saucepan, combine the soups, milk, sauerkraut and corned beef; cook and stir over medium heat for 8-10 minutes or until heated through. Add cheese; stir until melted. Top with croutons. YIELD: 8 SERVINGS (2 QUARTS).

Beer Cheese Soup

SHARON LOCK • FORMAN, NORTH DAKOTA

Onion, parsley, paprika and beer flavor this smooth, thick soup. A family friend used to invite us for Sunday supper and served this several times. It was so simple and good, I got the recipe for my daughter, who was just learning to cook at the time.

PREP/TOTAL TIME: 20 min.

2 tablespoons finely chopped onion
1/2 teaspoon butter
2 cans (10-3/4 ounces *each*) condensed cream of celery soup, undiluted
1 cup beer *or* nonalcoholic beer
1 cup milk
1 teaspoon Worcestershire sauce
1/2 teaspoon dried parsley flakes
1/4 teaspoon paprika
3/4 pound process cheese (Velveeta), cubed

In a large saucepan, saute onion in butter. Stir in the soup, beer, milk, Worcestershire sauce, parsley and paprika. Reduce heat; stir in cheese until melted. Heat through (do not boil). YIELD: 6 SERVINGS.

beer cheese soup

Grandma's Chicken 'n' Dumpling Soup

PAULETTE BALDA • PROPHETSTOWN, ILLINOIS

I've enjoyed making this rich soup for some 30 years. Every time I serve this home-style favorite, I think of my grandma, who was very special to me and was known as being a terrific cook.

PREP: 20 min. + cooling **COOK:** 2-3/4 hours

1	broiler/fryer chicken (3-1/2 to 4 pounds), cut up
2-1/4	quarts cold water
5	chicken bouillon cubes
6	whole peppercorns
3	whole cloves
1	can (10-3/4 ounces) condensed cream of chicken soup, undiluted
1	can (10-3/4 ounces) condensed cream of mushroom soup, undiluted
1-1/2	cups chopped carrots
1	cup fresh *or* frozen peas
1	cup chopped celery
1	cup chopped peeled potatoes
1/4	cup chopped onion
1-1/2	teaspoons seasoned salt
1/4	teaspoon pepper
1	bay leaf

DUMPLINGS:

2	cups all-purpose flour
4	teaspoons baking powder
1	teaspoon salt
1/4	teaspoon pepper
1	egg, beaten
2	tablespoons butter, melted
3/4	to 1 cup milk

Snipped fresh parsley, optional

Place chicken, water, bouillon, peppercorns and cloves in an 8-qt. Dutch oven or soup kettle. Cover and bring to a boil; skim foam. Reduce heat; cover and simmer 46-60 minutes or until chicken is tender. Strain broth; return to kettle.

Remove chicken and set aside until cool enough to handle. Remove meat from bones; discard bones and skin and cut chicken into chunks. Cool broth and skim off fat.

Return chicken to kettle with soups, vegetables and seasonings; bring to a boil. Reduce heat; cover and simmer for 1 hour. Uncover; increase heat to a gently boil. Discard bay leaf.

For dumplings, combine dry ingredients in a medium bowl. Stir in egg, butter and enough milk to make a moist stiff batter. Drop by teaspoonfuls into soup. Cover and cook without lifting the lid for 18-20 minutes. Sprinkle with parsley if desired. YIELD: 12 SERVINGS (3 QUARTS).

Hearty Hash Brown Soup

FRANCES RECTOR • VINTON, IOWA

Once folks take a spoonful of this soup that is chock-full of potatoes and ham, they will think you fussed. Because the recipe calls for frozen hash browns, it is really simple and fast to make.

PREP: 10 min. **COOK:** 30 min.

2	pounds frozen shredded hash brown potatoes
4	cups water
1	large onion, chopped
3/4	cup sliced celery
4	chicken bouillon cubes
1/2	teaspoon celery seed
1/4	teaspoon pepper
4	cans (10-3/4 ounces *each*) condensed cream of chicken soup, undiluted
1	quart milk
2	cups cubed fully cooked ham
1	tablespoon dried parsley flakes
1-1/2	teaspoons garlic salt
8	bacon strips, cooked and crumbled

In a Dutch oven or soup kettle, combine the first seven ingredients; bring to a boil. Reduce heat; cover and simmer for 20 minutes or until vegetables are tender. Mash vegetables with cooking liquid. Add soup and milk; stir until smooth. Add ham, parsley and garlic salt; simmer for 10 minutes or until heated through. Garnish with bacon. YIELD: 12-16 SERVINGS (4 QUARTS).

grandma's chicken 'n' dumpling soup

Sausage Corn Chowder

SHARON WALLACE • OMAHA, NEBRASKA

This hearty soup is a meal in itself when served with a salad and bread. For spicier flavor, I sometimes substitute Mexicorn for the whole kernel corn.

PREP/TOTAL TIME: 25 min.

2	packages (7 ounces *each*) pork *or* turkey breakfast sausage
2	cans (10-3/4 ounces *each*) condensed cream of chicken soup, undiluted
2-1/2	cups milk
2	cups fresh corn
2/3	cup sliced green onions
1/2	teaspoon hot pepper sauce
1	cup (4 ounces) shredded Swiss cheese

Crumble sausage into a large saucepan or Dutch oven; brown over medium heat. Drain. Add soup, milk, corn, green onions and hot pepper sauce. Cook until corn is tender. Reduce heat to low; add cheese and heat until melted. YIELD: 6-8 SERVING (2 QUARTS).

Cauliflower Ham Chowder

CARLA GARLOFF • BURNEY, CALIFORNIA

Even if you aren't crazy about cauliflower, you'll like this thick and chunky soup. My two daughters always did...and my husband and I love it, too. It's great to prepare when you have leftover ham.

PREP/TOTAL TIME: 25 min.

2	cups sliced fresh cauliflower
1	can (14-1/2 ounces) chicken broth
1	can (10-3/4 ounces) condensed cream of chicken soup, undiluted
1	cup half-and-half cream
1/8	teaspoon white pepper
2	tablespoons cornstarch
1/4	cup cold water
2	cups cubed fully cooked ham
Sliced green onion	

In a large saucepan, cook cauliflower in broth for 4 minutes or until crisp-tender. Stir in the soup, cream and pepper. Combine cornstarch and water until smooth; gradually stir into cauliflower mixture. Bring to a boil; cook and stir for 2 minutes or until thickened. Reduce heat. Add ham; cook and stir for 2 minutes or until heated through. Garnish with onion. YIELD: 6 SERVINGS.

chicken tortilla soup

Chicken Tortilla Soup

CAROLYN GRIFFIN • MACON, GEORGIA

Just a few additions to canned cream of chicken soup provide the comforting flavor found in this mock chicken dumpling soup. The chunks of chicken are nice and tender and you cannot tell that the dumplings are actually flour tortilla strips.

PREP/TOTAL TIME: 30 min.

1	can (10-3/4 ounces) condensed cream of chicken soup, undiluted
4	cups water
2	cups cubed cooked chicken
4	flour tortillas (6 inches), cut into 2-1/2-inch strips
Minced fresh parsley	

In a 3-qt. saucepan, bring the soup and water to a boil. Stir in the chicken and tortilla strips; reduce heat to medium-low. Cook, uncovered, for 25-30 minutes, stirring occasionally. Sprinkle with parsley. YIELD: 6 SERVINGS.

cooking tip

Keep a heavy-duty resealable plastic bag in the freezer to store soup ingredients. Whenever you have corn, peas, beans and other vegetables left over at dinner, put them in the bag. You can do the same with leftover chicken, turkey or ham.

broccoli potato soup

Broccoli Potato Soup

BARBARA BAKER • VALPARAISO, INDIANA

I rely on a few handy ingredients to make a can of soup taste just like homemade. The creamy mixture that results is hearty with broccoli and potato.

PREP/TOTAL TIME: 10 min.

2	cups fresh broccoli florets
1	small onion, thinly sliced
1	tablespoon butter
1	can (10-3/4 ounces) condensed cream of potato soup, undiluted
1	cup milk
1/2	cup water
3/4	teaspoon minced fresh basil *or* 1/4 teaspoon dried basil
1/4	teaspoon pepper
1/3	cup shredded cheddar cheese

In a large saucepan, saute broccoli and onion in butter until tender. Stir in soup, milk, water, basil and pepper; heat through. Add cheese; stir until melted. YIELD: 4 SERVINGS.

Enchilada Chicken Soup

CRISTIN FISCHER • BELLEVUE, NEBRASKA

Canned soups, bottled enchilada sauce and a few other convenience items make this restaurant-style soup one of my fast-to-fix favorites. Use mild green chilies if they suit your tastes, or try a spicier variety to give the soup even more kick.

PREP/TOTAL TIME: 10 min.

1	can (11 ounces) condensed fiesta nacho cheese soup, undiluted
1	can (10-3/4 ounces) condensed cream of chicken soup, undiluted
2-2/3	cups milk
1	can (10 ounces) chunk white chicken, drained
1	can (10 ounces) enchilada sauce
1	can (4 ounces) chopped green chilies
Sour cream	

In a large saucepan, combine the soups, milk, chicken, enchilada sauce and chilies; mix well. Cook until heated through. Serve with sour cream. YIELD: 7 SERVINGS.

Chicken & Bacon Chowder

NANCY SCHMIDT • DELHI, CALIFORNIA

The original recipe for this enticing chowder called for ground beef. One day I decided to add variety by using chicken instead. Everyone agreed they liked it even better. You're sure to enjoy it, too.

PREP: 15 min. **COOK:** 40 min.

1	pound sliced bacon
3	cups chopped celery
1/2	cup diced onion
4	cups cubed peeled potatoes
3	cups chicken broth
2	cups chopped carrots
3	cups cubed cooked chicken
2	cans (10-3/4 ounces *each*) condensed cream of mushroom soup, undiluted
2	cups half-and-half cream
1/2	teaspoon salt
1/2	teaspoon pepper

In a large soup kettle or Dutch oven, cook bacon until crisp. Drain, reserving 2 tablespoons drippings. Crumble bacon and set aside.

Saute celery and onion in drippings until tender. Add potatoes, broth and carrots; bring to a boil. Reduce heat; cover and simmer for 20 minutes or until vegetables are tender. Stir in remaining ingredients and heat through. YIELD: 12 SERVINGS (3 QUARTS).

cooking tip

Don't throw away leftover chicken broth—save it for later! Pour extra broth into an ice cube tray and freeze it. Then, the next time you're ready to make soup, pull out as many cubes as you need.

Cheesy Asparagus Soup

PATRICIA LOCKARD • ROCKFORD, MICHIGAN

Asparagus lovers will be delighted with this soup. It starts with lots of cooked fresh asparagus to which I add a can of cream of asparagus soup.

PREP/TOTAL TIME: 25 min.

3	pounds fresh asparagus, trimmed
1	small onion, chopped
2	cans (10-3/4 ounces *each*) condensed cream of asparagus soup, undiluted
2	soup cans milk
1	jar (4-1/2 ounces) sliced mushroom, drained
3	cups (12 ounces) shredded cheddar cheese

In a large kettle, cook asparagus and onion in a small amount of water until tender. Drain liquid. Add all remaining ingredients; heat over medium heat until the cheese is melted and the soup is hot.
YIELD: 8-10 SERVINGS.

In-a-Hurry Curry Soup

DENISE ELDER • HANOVER, ONTARIO

Curry makes this speedy soup so delicious. I just open a few cans, and I have a quick, filling meal in minutes. The wonderful aroma brings my family to the table before I even have a chance to call them.

PREP/TOTAL TIME: 10 min.

1	cup chopped onion
3/4	teaspoon curry powder
2	tablespoons butter
2	chicken bouillon cubes
1	cup hot water
1	can (14-1/2 ounces) diced tomatoes, undrained
1	can (10-3/4 ounces) condensed cream of celery soup, undiluted
1	cup half-and-half cream
1	can (5 ounces) white chicken, drained

In a 3-qt. saucepan, saute onion and curry powder in butter until onion is tender. Dissolve bouillon in water; add to the saucepan. Stir in remaining ingredients; heat through. YIELD: ABOUT 5 SERVINGS.

Broccoli Wild Rice Soup

MARTHA POLLOCK • OREGONIA, OHIO

Colorful and comforting, this inviting meal-in-a-bowl relies on readily available ingredients I usually have on hand. I like topping the individual servings with sliced almonds for a delicious, nutty crunch.

PREP: 5 min. **COOK:** 30 min.

5	cups water
1	package (6 ounces) long grain and wild rice mix
1	can (10-3/4 ounces) reduced-fat reduced-sodium condensed cream of chicken soup, undiluted
1-1/2	cups fat-free milk
1	package (8 ounces) fat-free cream cheese, cubed
1/4	teaspoon salt
3	cups frozen chopped broccoli, thawed
1	large carrot, shredded
1/4	cup sliced almonds, toasted

In a large saucepan, combine the water and rice mix with contents of seasoning packet; bring to a boil. Reduce heat; cover and simmer for 20 minutes. Add the soup, milk, cream cheese and salt; stir until cheese is melted. Add broccoli and carrot; cook over medium-low heat for 5-6 minutes or until vegetables and rice are tender. Sprinkle soup with almonds.
YIELD: 6 SERVINGS.

broccoli wild rice soup

CHAPTER 3
Sunday Brunch

Sunday Brunch Casserole

ROY LYON • COUPEVILLE, WASHINGTON

My father was a chef, and this was one of his favorite recipes. Whenever it's served today in my home, it never fails to bring back fond memories of a table laden with food and encircled with family and friends enjoying the aromas, tastes and laughter.

PREP: 15 min. **BAKE:** 1 hour

6	slices sourdough bread
3	to 4 tablespoons butter, softened
2	cups (8 ounces) shredded cheddar cheese
1	pound bulk pork sausage, cooked and drained
1/2	medium sweet red pepper, cut into thin strips
1/4	cup sliced green onion tops
3	eggs
1	can (10-3/4 ounces) condensed cream of asparagus soup, undiluted
2	cups milk
1/4	cup white wine *or* chicken broth
1/2	teaspoon Dijon mustard
1/4	teaspoon pepper

Remove and discard crust from bread if desired. Butter bread; cube and place in a greased 13-in. x 9-in. x 2-in. baking dish. Sprinkle with the cheese, sausage, red pepper and onions in order given.

In a large bowl, beat eggs. Add the soup, milk, wine, mustard and pepper. Pour over bread mixture; cover and refrigerate overnight.

Remove from the refrigerator 30 minutes before baking. Bake, uncovered, at 300° for 1 hour or until a knife comes out clean. Let stand for 5 minutes before cutting. YIELD: 8-10 SERVINGS.

Eggs Ahoy

MARTHA CREECH • KINSTON, NORTH CAROLINA

This dish is not quite eggs Benedict, but it's good. A can of cream of celery soup is the simple substitute for traditional hollandaise sauce in this quick-and-easy version.

PREP/TOTAL TIME: 15 min.

2	tablespoons chopped green pepper
2	tablespoons butter, *divided*
1	can (10-3/4 ounces) condensed cream of celery soup, undiluted
1/4	cup milk

sunday brunch casserole

3	English muffins, split and toasted
12	bacon strips, cooked
6	poached eggs

In a saucepan, saute green pepper in 1 tablespoon butter until tender. Add the soup and milk; cook and stir until heated through. Spread remaining butter over muffin halves. Place two bacon strips on each half; top each with a poached egg and the soup mixture. YIELD: 3 SERVINGS.

Hobo Hash

LINDA HENDERSHOTT • ST. JOSEPH, MICHIGAN

I came up with this recipe one day when I didn't have many groceries in the house. My kids named it Hobo Hash because it didn't have a lot in it and could be cooked in one pan.

PREP/TOTAL TIME: 30 min.

1/2	pound sliced bacon, diced
1	medium onion, chopped
1	cup sliced fresh mushrooms
5	medium potatoes, peeled, cubed and cooked
1	can (10.-3/4 ounces) condensed cream of mushroom soup, undiluted

In a large skillet, cook bacon over medium heat until crisp. Remove bacon to paper towels to drain, reserving 3 tablespoons drippings.

Saute onion and mushrooms in drippings until onion is tender. Stir in the potatoes and soup. Simmer, uncovered, for 5 minutes or until heated through. Sprinkle with bacon. YIELD: 4 SERVINGS.

baked stuffed eggs

Add soup and sour cream; mix well. Pour half into an ungreased 11-in. x 7-in. x 2-in. baking pan.

Arrange stuffed eggs over the sauce. Spoon remaining sauce on top. Sprinkle with cheese and paprika. Cover and refrigerate overnight.

Remove from the refrigerator 30 minutes before baking. Bake, uncovered, at 350° for 25-30 minutes or until heated through. Serve immediately. YIELD: 6-8 SERVINGS.

Holiday Ham Ring

VIRGINIA ALVERSON • MILROY, INDIANA

I always seem to have one of these delicious ham rings in the freezer to share with neighbors during difficult times. Folks say its country-style taste reminds them of their grandma's cooking.

PREP: 15 min. BAKE: 1 hour

1-1/2	pounds fully cooked ham, ground
1/2	pound ground pork
3/4	cup graham cracker crumbs
3/4	cup milk
1	egg
1/4	teaspoon ground allspice
1/4	teaspoon pepper
1/2	cup condensed cream of tomato soup, undiluted
1/4	cup vinegar
1/4	cup packed brown sugar
1/2	teaspoon prepared mustard

Combine the first seven ingredients; mix well. On a 15-in. x 10-in. x 1-in. baking pan, shape meat mixture into a 9-1/2-in.-diameter ring. Combine soup, vinegar, brown sugar and mustard; pour half over ham ring.

Bake, uncovered, at 350° for 30 minutes. Pour remaining soup mixture over the top; bake 30 minutes longer or until a meat thermometer reads 160°-170°. YIELD: 8 SERVINGS.

Potato Egg Supper

ROSEMARY FLEXMAN • WAUKESHA, WISCONSIN

I serve this convenient, all-in-one casserole for breakfast or dinner! I've taken it to church suppers many times, where it's always a hit.

PREP: 20 min. BAKE: 30 min.

4	cups diced cooked peeled potatoes
8	bacon strips, cooked and crumbled
4	hard-cooked eggs, sliced

Baked Stuffed Eggs

LORRAINE BYLSMA • EUTIS, FLORIDA

Lucky for me, the man I married was very patient. As a young bride, I could hardly boil water! But I have perfected many dishes over the years. And this make-ahead egg dish, which is wonderful for brunches and potlucks, is one of them.

PREP: 15 min. + chilling BAKE: 25 min.

STUFFED EGGS:

8	hard-cooked eggs
3	to 4 tablespoons sour cream
2	teaspoons prepared mustard
1/2	teaspoon salt

SAUCE:

1/2	cup chopped onion
2	tablespoons butter
1	can (10-3/4 ounces) condensed cream of mushroom soup, undiluted
1	cup (8 ounces) sour cream
1/2	cup shredded cheddar cheese
1/2	teaspoon paprika

Slice eggs in half lengthwise; remove yolks and set whites aside. In a bowl, mash yolks with a fork. Add sour cream, mustard and salt; mix well. Stuff or pipe into egg whites; set aside.

In a saucepan, saute onion in butter until tender.

1   can (10-3/4 ounces) condensed cream
       of mushroom soup, undiluted
1/2 cup milk
1   small onion, chopped
1   tablespoon chopped green pepper
1   tablespoon chopped sweet red pepper
1   cup (4 ounces) shredded cheddar
       cheese

Place half of the potatoes in a greased 2-qt. baking dish. Top with bacon, eggs and remaining potatoes. In a saucepan, combine the soup, milk, onion and peppers. Cook over medium heat until heated through. Pour over the potatoes.

Cover and bake at 350° for 20 minutes. Uncover; sprinkle with cheese. Bake 10-15 minutes longer or until heated through. YIELD: 4 SERVINGS.

Asparagus Chicken Crepes

ANGELA LEINENBACH • MECHANICSVILLE, VIRGINIA

With a saucy ham and asparagus filling, these savory crepes make a lovely dinner. They are a wonderful change of pace from everyday fare.

PREP: 40 min. + chilling **COOK:** 30 min.

2   eggs
3/4 cup milk
1/2 cup all-purpose flour
3/4 teaspoon sugar
1/2 cup condensed cream of chicken soup,
       undiluted
1   teaspoon Worcestershire sauce
Dash ground nutmeg

cooking tip

To keep unused asparagus fresh longer, place the cut stems in a flower vase or similar container filled with cold water. Keep the asparagus in the refrigerator, changing the water at least once every three days.

1   cup chopped cooked chicken
1   cup cut fresh *or* frozen asparagus,
       thawed
1/3 cup chopped fully cooked ham
1/2 cup grated Parmesan cheese, *divided*
1/2 cup heavy whipping cream, whipped
1/3 cup mayonnaise

For crepe batter, beat eggs and milk in a small mixing bowl. Combine flour and sugar; add to egg mixture and mix well. Cover and refrigerate for 1 hour.

Heat a lightly greased 8-in. nonstick skillet; pour 3 tablespoons batter into the center of skillet. Lift and tilt pan to evenly coat bottom. Cook until top appears dry; turn and cook 15-20 seconds longer. Remove to a wire rack. Repeat with remaining batter, greasing skillet as needed. When cool, stack crepes with waxed paper between.

In a small bowl, combine the cream of chicken soup, Worcestershire sauce and nutmeg. Set aside 1/4 cup. Add the chicken, asparagus and ham to remaining soup mixture. Spoon 2 tablespoonfuls over each crepe; roll up tightly. Place seam side down in a greased 9-in. square baking pan. Spoon reserved soup mixture over crepes. Sprinkle with 1/4 cup Parmesan cheese.

Cover and bake at 375° for 20-25 minutes. Gradually fold cream into mayonnaise. Spread over crepes. Sprinkle with remaining Parmesan. Broil 6 in. from the heat for 3-5 minutes or until bubbly and golden brown. YIELD: 4 SERVINGS.

asparagus chicken crepes

Night Before Casserole

MARION KIRST • TROY, MICHIGAN

Although my Aunt Edith served a huge pancake breakfast with generous helpings of bacon or sausage, she always made this hearty casserole, too. The bread, egg and cheese combo came out of the oven light and puffy, and your fork glided through it.

PREP: 10 min. **BAKE:** 1 hour

- 12 slices white bread, crusts removed
- 6 to 8 tablespoons butter, softened
- 6 slices deluxe American cheese
- 6 slices boiled *or* baked ham
- Prepared mustard
- 4 eggs, beaten
- 3 cups milk
- Chopped fresh parsley

MUSHROOM SAUCE:
- 1 can (10-3/4 ounces) condensed cream of mushroom soup, undiluted
- 1/3 cup milk
- Dash Worcestershire sauce

Spread bread with butter. Place six slices in a greased 13-in. x 9-in. x 2-in. baking dish. Top each bread slice with a slice of cheese and ham. Brush with mustard. Place the remaining bread slices, buttered side up, over mustard. Beat eggs and milk; pour over all. Cover and refrigerate overnight.

Remove from the refrigerator 30 minutes before baking. Bake at 325° for 50-60 minutes or until a knife comes out clean. Let stand 5 minutes before serving. Meanwhile, heat sauce ingredients and keep warm. Garnish with parsley; serve with the mushroom sauce. YIELD: 12 SERVINGS.

night before casserole

Sausage, Hominy & Egg Brunch

MARY ELLEN ANDREWS • NEWVILLE, ALABAMA

This egg specialty spotlights hominy, which is a basic ingredient in Southern cooking. It's especially nice to serve on cold winter days for brunch or even supper.

PREP: 15 min. **BAKE:** 30 min.

- 1 pound bulk hot pork sausage
- 6 hard-cooked eggs, sliced
- 2 cans (15-1/2 ounces *each*) yellow hominy, drained
- 1 can (10-3/4 ounces) condensed cream of mushroom soup, undiluted
- 1 cup (8 ounces) sour cream
- 1/4 teaspoon Worcestershire sauce
- 1 cup (4 ounces) shredded cheddar cheese
- 1 cup soft bread crumbs
- 3 tablespoons butter, melted

In a skillet, cook sausage until no longer pink; drain. Spoon into a 2-1/2-qt. ungreased baking dish. Cover with layers of eggs and hominy. Combine soup, sour cream and Worcestershire sauce; spread over hominy. Sprinkle with cheese. Combine bread crumbs and butter; sprinkle over top. Bake, uncovered, at 325° for 30-35 minutes or until bubbly and golden brown. YIELD: 6-8 SERVINGS.

Curried Eggs in Shrimp Sauce

M. BEATRICE MANN • VERNON, VERMONT

In this tasty brunch dish, I like to dress up ordinary hard-cooked eggs with a special shrimp sauce. This hot dish is handy because you can assemble it the day before and bake it the next morning.

Prep: 40 min. **BAKE:** 15 min.

- 3 tablespoons butter, *divided*
- 2 tablespoons all-purpose flour
- 1 can (10-3/4 ounces) condensed cream of shrimp soup, undiluted
- 1 cup milk
- 1/2 cup shredded cheddar cheese
- 1/2 pound frozen cooked small shrimp, thawed and chopped
- 12 hard-cooked eggs
- 1/2 cup mayonnaise
- 1/4 teaspoon curry powder

1/4	teaspoon ground mustard
1/4	teaspoon paprika
1/8	teaspoon salt
1	cup soft bread crumbs

In a large saucepan, melt 2 tablespoons butter; whisk in flour until smooth. Gradually add soup and milk. Bring to a boil; cook and stir over medium heat for 2 minutes or until thickened. Remove from the heat; stir in cheese until melted. Stir in shrimp.

Pour 2 cups of sauce into a greased 13-in. x 9-in. x 2-in. baking dish; set remaining sauce aside. Cut eggs in half lengthwise; arrange whites over sauce. In a bowl, mash yolks. Stir in the mayonnaise, curry powder, mustard, paprika and salt. Spoon into egg whites. Top with reserved sauce.

Melt the remaining butter; toss with bread crumbs. Sprinkle over the top. Bake, uncovered, at 350° for 15-20 minutes or until heated through. YIELD: 12 SERVINGS.

cheddar broccoli quiche

Hard-Cooked Egg Casserole

LOIS HORN • BEAUFORT, SOUTH CAROLINA

My husband's mother was a wonderful cook from Wisconsin. This was a favorite breakfast casserole of her children back then, and my kids loved it just as much when they were growing up, too.

PREP: 15 min. BAKE: 40 min.

4-1/2	teaspoons all-purpose flour
2	cups milk
1	can (10-3/4 ounces) condensed cream of mushroom soup, undiluted
1/2	pound fresh mushrooms, sliced
1/4	cup butter, *divided*
1	cup dry bread crumbs
1-1/2	pounds cubed fully cooked ham
4	hard-cooked eggs, chopped

In a saucepan, combine flour and milk until smooth; stir in mushroom soup. Bring to a boil; cook and stir for 2 minutes or until thickened. In a skillet, saute mushrooms in 2 tablespoons butter until tender. Add to the sauce. In the same skillet, brown bread crumbs in the remaining butter.

In a greased 2-qt. baking dish, layer half of the ham, eggs and buttered bread crumbs. Pour half of the mushroom sauce evenly over the top. Layer with remaining ham, eggs, sauce and bread crumbs. Cover and bake at 375° for 40-45 minutes or until heated through. YIELD: 6 SERVINGS.

Cheddar Broccoli Quiche

BARBARA CUSIMANO • MANCHESTER, CONNECTICUT

This savory quiche is a snap to create with a convenient pastry shell crust and a can of broccoli and cheese soup. Pair it with fresh fruit, such as sliced melon, strawberries or kiwi, for a complete meal. I find this dish is perfect for special occasions.

PREP: 10 min. BAKE: 35 min.

1	pastry shell (9 inches), baked
1	cup (4 ounces) shredded cheddar cheese, *divided*
6	eggs
1	can (10-3/4 ounces) condensed cream of broccoli and cheese soup, undiluted
2/3	cup milk

Sprinkle pastry shell with 1/2 cup cheese. In a large bowl, combine the eggs, soup and milk. Pour into crust. Cover edges loosely with foil.

Bake at 350° for 30 minutes. Sprinkle top with remaining cheese; bake quiche 5-10 minutes longer or until a knife inserted near the center comes out clean. Let the quiche stand for 5 minutes before cutting. YIELD: 6-8 SERVINGS.

sausage & broccoli bake

bowl, combine the eggs, soup and milk. Pour over sausage mixture. Bake, uncovered, at 375° for 25 minutes. Sprinkle with French-fried onions. Bake for 3-5 minutes longer or until a knife inserted near the center comes out clean. YIELD: 6-8 SERVINGS.

Hash 'n' Eggs

DOROTHY SMITH • EL DORADO, ARKANSAS

I turn corned beef and cooked potatoes from dinner into a hearty morning meal to be enjoyed the next day.

PREP/TOTAL TIME: 25 min.

2	tablespoons butter
4	cups cubed cooked potatoes
1	can (10-3/4 ounces) condensed cream of celery soup, undiluted
1/4	cup milk
1	teaspoon prepared mustard
1/4	teaspoon hot pepper sauce
1-1/2	cups cubed cooked corned beef (8 ounces)
4	eggs

Pepper to taste

In a skillet, melt butter over medium heat. Add potatoes and cook for 2 minutes, stirring often. Stir in the soup, milk, mustard and hot pepper sauce; cook until heated through. Stir in the corned beef. Reduce heat to low. Make four wells in potato mixture; break an egg into each well. Cover and cook for 10-15 minutes or until eggs are completely set. Add pepper to taste. YIELD: 4 SERVINGS.

Swiss Woods Souffle

WERNER AND DEBRAH MOSIMANN, LITITZ, PENNSYLVANIA

We developed this eye-opening recipe to serve at breakfast to the guests at our bed and breakfast.

PREP: 15 min. **BAKE:** 45 min.

8	to 10 slices bread, torn in pieces
5	eggs
2	cups milk, *divided*
1/2	teaspoon ground mustard
1/4	teaspoon salt
1/4	teaspoon pepper
1	pound bulk pork sausage
1	can (10-3/4 ounces) condensed cream of mushroom soup, undiluted *or* 1 cup thick homemade white sauce with 1/2 cup sauteed mushrooms

Sausage & Broccoli Bake

ROBIN MOHERMAN • ASHLAND, OHIO

I make this easy meat and veggie bake often because it provides plenty of delicious leftovers for later. It goes over big as a featured entree for a brunch buffet.

PREP: 20 min. **BAKE:** 30 min.

3	cups frozen chopped broccoli
1	pound bulk Italian sausage
3	cups seasoned salad croutons
2	cups (8 ounces) shredded sharp cheddar cheese
4	eggs, lightly beaten
1	can (10-3/4 ounces) condensed cream of broccoli soup, undiluted
1-1/3	cups milk
1	can (2.8 ounces) French-fried onions

Cook broccoli according to package directions; drain and set aside. In a large skillet, cook sausage over medium heat until the meat is no longer pink; drain. Add the broccoli, croutons and cheese.

Transfer to a greased 2-qt. baking dish. In a large

1/2   cup shredded Gruyere cheese
1/2   cup shredded Emmenthaler Swiss cheese

Arrange bread in an ungreased 13-in. x 9-in. x 2-in. baking dish. Whisk together the eggs, 1-1/2 cups milk and seasonings; pour over bread and set aside.

Meanwhile, in a large skillet, cook sausage over medium heat until no longer pink; drain. Spoon over bread. Combine the soup, cheeses and remaining milk; spread over sausage.

Bake, uncovered, at 350° for 45-50 minutes or until golden brown. Let stand for 5 minutes before serving. YIELD: 6-8 SERVINGS.

Christmas Brunch Casserole

MARY ECKLER • LOUISVILLE, KENTUCKY

No one leaves the table hungry when I serve this savory casserole filled with sausage, rice, eggs and cheese. What I like as much as the taste is that I can prepare it ahead of time.

PREP: 20 min. BAKE: 55 min.

2   pounds bulk pork sausage
1   large onion, chopped
2   cups cooked rice
3   cups crisp rice cereal
3   cups (12 ounces) shredded cheddar cheese
6   eggs
2   cans (10-3/4 ounces *each*) condensed cream of celery soup, undiluted
1/2   cup milk

In a skillet, cook sausage and onion over medium heat until meat is no longer pink; drain. Place in a lightly greased 13-in. x 9-in. x 2-in. baking dish.

Top sausage mixture with the rice, cereal and cheddar cheese. In a bowl, beat the eggs, soup and milk. Spread over top.

Bake, uncovered, at 350° for 55-60 minutes or until a knife inserted near the center comes out clean. Let stand for 5 minutes before cutting. Refrigerate any leftovers. YIELD: 12 SERVINGS.

Cheese 'n' Ham Strata

ILENE HARRINGTON • NIPOMO, CALIFORNIA

We love to hold potluck meals at our church, and this is the dish I make for those get-togethers. Chock-full of ham and cheese, it always receives rave reviews.

PREP: 20 min. + chilling BAKE: 40 min. + standing

5   cups cubed bread, *divided*
2   cups cubed fully cooked ham
1/4   cup chopped green pepper
2   tablespoons chopped onion
2   cups (8 ounces) shredded cheddar cheese
1   cup (4 ounces) shredded pepper Jack cheese
1   can (10-3/4 ounces) condensed cream of chicken soup, undiluted
1-1/3   cups milk
4   eggs
1   cup mayonnaise
1/2   teaspoon pepper
Dash cayenne pepper
2   tablespoons butter, melted
2   tablespoons minced fresh parsley

Place 3-1/2 cups bread in a greased 13-in. x 9-in. x 2-in. baking dish. Top with ham, green pepper and onion; sprinkle with cheeses. In a large bowl, combine soup and milk. Stir in the eggs, mayonnaise, pepper and cayenne. Pour soup mixture over cheeses. Toss remaining bread cubes with butter. Sprinkle over soup mixture. Cover and refrigerate for 8 hours or overnight.

Remove from the refrigerator 30 minutes before baking. Bake, uncovered, at 350° for 40-45 minutes or until a knife inserted near the center comes out clean. Sprinkle with parsley. Let stand for 5 minutes before serving. YIELD: 8-10 SERVINGS.

EDITOR'S NOTE: Reduced-fat or fat-free mayonnaise is not recommended for this recipe.

cheese 'n' ham strata

Sausage Hash Brown Bake

ESTHER WRINKLES • VANZANT, MISSOURI

Pork sausage is sandwiched between layers of hash browns flavored with cream of chicken soup and French onion dip. Cheddar cheese tops the all-in-one breakfast casserole.

PREP: 15 min. **BAKE:** 55 min.

2	pounds bulk pork sausage
2	cups (8 ounces) shredded cheddar cheese, *divided*
1	can (10-3/4 ounces) condensed cream of chicken soup, undiluted
1	cup (8 ounces) sour cream
1	carton (8 ounces) French onion dip
1	cup chopped onion
1/4	cup chopped green pepper
1/4	cup chopped sweet red pepper
1/8	teaspoon pepper
1	package (30 ounces) frozen shredded hash brown potatoes, thawed

In a large skillet, cook sausage over medium heat until no longer pink; drain on paper towels. In a large bowl, combine 1-3/4 cups cheese and the next seven ingredients; fold in potatoes.

Spread half into a greased shallow 3-qt. baking dish. Top with sausage and remaining potato mixture. Sprinkle with remaining cheese. Cover and bake at 350° for 45 minutes. Uncover; bake 10 minutes longer or until heated through. YIELD: 10-12 SERVINGS.

sausage hash brown bake

Bacon Mushroom Bake

TAMMI EVANS • BATTLE CREEK, MICHIGAN

I'm the mother of two teenagers, co-owner of a plumbing business with my husband, plus I work part-time, so a tried-and-true recipe like this is treasured.

PREP: 15 min. **BAKE:** 40 min.

18	eggs
1-1/2	cups half-and-half cream, *divided*
1	can (10-3/4 ounces) condensed cream of chicken soup, undiluted
1/2	pound fresh mushrooms, sliced
2	tablespoons butter
1	pound sliced bacon, cooked and crumbled
2	cups (8 ounces) shredded cheddar cheese

In a mixing bowl, beat the eggs with 1 cup cream. Pour into a lightly greased large skillet. Cook and stir over medium heat until eggs are set. Combine the soup and remaining cream; set aside.

In another skillet, saute mushrooms in butter until tender. In an ungreased 13-in. x 9-in. x 2-in. baking dish, layer the eggs, bacon, mushrooms and cheese. Pour soup mixture over top.

Bake, uncovered, at 350° for 40 minutes or until heated through. Let dish stand for 5 minutes before serving. YIELD: 10-12 SERVINGS.

Eggs Delmonico

EDIE FARM • FARMINGTON, NEW MEXICO

These creamed eggs on toast get their rich, comforting flavor from a can of cream of mushroom soup mixed with melted cheddar cheese.

PREP/TOTAL TIME: 10 min.

1	can (10-3/4 ounces) condensed cream of mushroom *or* cream of chicken soup, undiluted
1/2	cup shredded cheddar cheese
3	hard-cooked eggs, sliced
1	tablespoon finely chopped pimientos
4	pieces toast *or* 2 English muffins, split and toasted

Paprika *or* minced fresh parsley

In a saucepan, heat soup over medium heat until hot and bubbly. Reduce heat; stir in cheese. Cook and stir until cheese is melted. Fold in eggs and pimientos; cook until heated through. Serve over toast or English muffins. Garnish with paprika or parsley. YIELD: 2 SERVINGS.

Ham 'n' Egg Tortilla Bake

LAUREN BUDWEG • OBERLIN, OHIO

This recipe came about one day when I needed to make my husband's lunch and we were out of bread. This is now one of his favorites. It's also a great brunch casserole.

PREP: 25 min. **BAKE:** 20 min.

1	cup sliced fresh mushrooms
1	medium onion, chopped
1/2	cup chopped green pepper
1/4	cup butter, cubed
6	eggs
1/4	cup milk
1/4	teaspoon pepper
1	cup cubed fully cooked ham
1	can (10-3/4 ounces) condensed cream of mushroom soup, undiluted
10	flour tortillas (8 inches), warmed
1-1/2	cups (6 ounces) shredded cheddar cheese

In a large skillet, saute the mushrooms, onion and green pepper in butter until tender. Meanwhile, in a large bowl, whisk together the eggs, milk and pepper; add the ham. Pour into the skillet. Cook and stir over medium heat until eggs are completely set.

In a greased 13-in. x 9-in. x 2-in. baking dish, spread half of the soup. Place 3 tablespoons egg mixture down the center of each tortilla; sprinkle each with 1 tablespoon cheese. Roll up and place seam side down over soup.

Spread remaining soup over tortillas. Sprinkle with remaining cheese. Bake, uncovered, at 350° for 20-25 minutes or until the tortillas are heated through. YIELD: 5 SERVINGS.

Fast and Flavorful Eggs

MICHELE CHRISTMAN • SIDNEY, ILLINOIS

With a short ingredient list and cooking time, this dish is one of my favorite ways to prepare eggs. And with my busy schedule, I need all the free time I can get!

PREP/TOTAL TIME: 25 min.

1/4	cup chopped green pepper
1	tablespoon butter
6	eggs, lightly beaten
1	can (10-3/4 ounces) condensed cream of chicken soup, undiluted, *divided*

ham mushroom pie

3/4	teaspoon salt
1/2	teaspoon pepper
6	bacon strips, cooked and crumbled
1/2	cup milk

In a skillet, saute green pepper in butter until tender. Combine eggs, 1/2 cup soup, salt and pepper. Add to skillet; cook and stir gently until the eggs are set. Stir in bacon. For sauce, heat milk and remaining soup; stir until smooth. Serve sauce over eggs.
YIELD: 3-4 SERVINGS.

Ham Mushroom Pie

HOWIE WIENER • SPRING HILL, FLORIDA

This brunch specialty was given to me by my grandmother, who loved making fast and delicious meals. Even the most finicky eaters enjoy the layers of ham and egg in this quick-to-fix and inexpensive dish.

PREP: 15 min. **BAKE:** 35 min.

1	boneless ham steak (about 1 pound)
1	pastry shell (9 inches), baked
2/3	cup condensed cream of mushroom soup, undiluted
2/3	cup sour cream
3	eggs, lightly beaten
2	tablespoons minced chives

Dash pepper

Cut ham to fit the bottom of pastry shell; place ham in shell. In a bowl, combine the remaining ingredients; mix well. Pour mixture over ham. Cover edges loosely with foil.

Bake pie at 425° for 35-40 minutes or until a knife inserted near the center comes out clean.
YIELD: 6 SERVINGS.

Country Meat Loaf

JIM HOPKINS • WHITTIER, CALIFORNIA

This mouth-watering meat loaf has a comforting combination of beef, veal and pork and, for a change, is held together with corn bread stuffing.

PREP: 10 min. **BAKE:** 1-1/2 hours

- 2　eggs
- 1　can (10-3/4 ounces) condensed cream of celery soup, undiluted
- 1/2　teaspoon pepper
- 1　package (6 ounces) corn bread stuffing mix
- 1-1/2　pounds ground beef
- 1/2　pound ground veal
- 1/4　pound ground pork

In a large bowl, beat eggs. Add soup, pepper and stuffing mix. Combine beef, veal and pork; crumble over egg mixture and mix well.

Press meat mixture into a 9-in. x 5-in. x 3-in. loaf pan. Bake at 350° for 1-1/2 hours or until no pink remains. Drain. YIELD: 6-8 SERVINGS.

Beefy Broccoli Pie

BARB VAN DER HUEST • HOLLAND, MICHIGAN

This broccoli and ground beef pie uses a convenient refrigerated crescent roll crust for a no-fuss meal. Add a tossed salad and dinner's ready in a jiffy.

PREP: 15 min. **BAKE:** 25 min.

- 1　pound ground beef
- 1/4　cup chopped onion
- 1　package (10 ounces) frozen cut broccoli, cooked and drained
- 1　can (10-3/4 ounces) condensed cream of mushroom soup, undiluted
- 2　tubes (8 ounces *each*) refrigerated crescent rolls, *divided*
- 2　cups (8 ounces) shredded cheddar cheese

In a large skillet, cook beef and onion over medium heat until meat is no longer pink; drain. Add broccoli and soup.

Unroll one tube of crescent rolls. Press into a greased 13-in. x 9-in. x 2-in. baking pan. Seal seams and perforations. Top with meat mixture. Sprinkle with cheese. Unroll remaining crescent dough and place over meat mixture; seal seams and perforations.

Bake, uncovered, at 350° for 25 minutes or until golden brown. YIELD: 6-8 SERVINGS.

dijon mushroom beef

Dijon Mushroom Beef

JUDITH MCGHAN • PERRY HALL, MARYLAND

Coated in a mild Dijon mustard sauce, the tender beef strips and sliced mushrooms in this dish are delicious over noodles or rice. This was a hit with my family when I served it with fresh, steamed asparagus.

PREP/TOTAL TIME: 20 min.

- 1/2　pound fresh mushrooms, sliced
- 1　medium onion, sliced
- 2　teaspoons olive oil
- 1　pound boneless beef sirloin steak, thinly sliced
- 1　can (10-3/4 ounces) condensed cream of mushroom soup, undiluted
- 3/4　cup milk
- 2　tablespoons Dijon mustard

Hot cooked yolk-free noodles, optional

In a large nonstick skillet, saute mushrooms and onion in oil until tender. Remove and set aside. In the same skillet, cook beef until no longer pink. Add the soup, milk, mustard and mushroom mixture. Bring to a boil. Reduce heat; cook and stir until thickened. Serve over hot cooked noodles if desired. YIELD: 4 SERVINGS.

cooking tip

Use leftover meat loaf in pizzas, soups and stews. Place thick slices into individual freezer bags. Then, thaw the number of slices you need, cube and add to the recipe.

cheesy spaghetti bake

Cheesy Spaghetti Bake

SUE BRAUNSCHWEIG • DELAFIELD, WISCONSIN

With all the favorite ingredients of spaghetti and meat sauce, this recipe makes two hearty, family-style casseroles. It is a great dish for entertaining.

PREP: 45 min. **BAKE:** 40 min.

1	pound uncooked spaghetti, broken into 3-inch pieces
4	pounds ground beef
2	large onions, chopped
1	large green pepper, chopped
4	cups milk
4	cans (10-3/4 ounces *each*) condensed tomato soup, undiluted
2	cans (10-3/4 ounces *each*) condensed cream of mushroom soup, undiluted
4	cups (16 ounces) shredded sharp cheddar cheese, *divided*

Cook spaghetti according to package directions. Drain and place in two greased 13-in. x 9-in. x 2-in. baking dishes; set aside.

In two Dutch ovens or large kettles, cook the beef, onions and green pepper over medium heat until meat is no longer pink; drain. To each pot, add 2 cups of milk, two cans of tomato soup, one can of mushroom soup and 1 cup of cheese. Bring to a boil.

Spoon meat mixture over spaghetti (spaghetti will absorb liquid during baking). Sprinkle with remaining cheese. Bake, uncovered, at 350° for 40-45 minutes or until bubbly and top is lightly browned. YIELD: 2 CASSEROLES (12 SERVINGS EACH).

Hearty Hash Brown Dinner

MARGE BERG • GIBBON, MINNESOTA

At my home, this meal-in-one with vegetables and ground beef is frequent fare. It's ideal when you have a crowd to feed. French-fried onions sprinkled on after cooking create a crispy topping.

PREP: 15 min. **COOK:** 4-1/2 hours

3	cups frozen shredded hash brown potatoes, thawed
1/2	teaspoon salt
1/4	teaspoon pepper
1	pound ground beef
1/2	cup chopped onion
1	package (16 ounces) frozen California-blend vegetables
1	can (10-3/4 ounces) condensed cream of chicken soup, undiluted
1	cup milk
12	ounces process cheese (Velveeta), cubed
1	can (2.8 ounces) French-fried onions

Place potatoes in a lightly greased 5-qt. slow cooker; sprinkle with salt and pepper. In a large skillet, cook beef and onion over medium heat until meat is no longer pink; drain. Spoon over potatoes. Top with vegetables. Combine soup and milk; pour over vegetables. Cover and cook on low for 4 to 4-1/2 hours.

Top with cheese; cover and cook 30 minutes longer or until cheese is melted. Just before serving, sprinkle with French-fried onions. YIELD: 4 SERVINGS.

Meatballs with Rice

MINA DYCK • BOISSEVAIN, MANITOBA

A pound of ground beef goes a long way in this recipe. I especially like to take it to potluck suppers.

PREP: 15 min. **BAKE:** 1 hour 20 min.

1	pound ground beef
1/2	cup rolled oats
1-1/2	teaspoons salt, *divided*
1/2	teaspoon pepper
1/2	teaspoon celery salt
1	teaspoon dried parsley flakes
1	cup uncooked rice
1-1/2	cups sliced celery
1	large onion, chopped
1	can (4 ounces) mushroom stems and pieces, drained

2   cans (10-3/4 ounces *each*) condensed cream of asparagus soup, undiluted
2   cups water

In a mixing bowl, combine the ground beef, oats, 1/2 teaspoon salt, pepper, celery salt and parsley. Shape by tablespoonfuls into meatballs. Place meatballs on a greased rack in a shallow baking pan. Bake at 400° for 18 to 20 minutes or until browned.

Meanwhile, combine rice, celery, onion, mushrooms, soup, water and remaining salt.

Transfer meatballs to a greased 3-qt. casserole; pour soup mixture over. Cover and bake at 350° degrees for 1 hour or until liquid is absorbed and rice is tender. YIELD: 6-8 SERVINGS.

Mushroom Burger Pockets

ROSE SADOWSKY • DICKINSON, NORTH DAKOTA

These savory, handheld pockets are favored by my husband and sons during combining season. I always make sure I have a warm batch waiting for them to grab and eat when they are on the run.

PREP: 30 min. + rising **BAKE:** 20 min.

1-1/2   pounds ground beef
1   can (10-3/4 ounces) condensed cream of mushroom soup, undiluted
1   can (4 ounces) mushroom stems and pieces, drained
1   medium onion, chopped
1   tablespoon Worcestershire sauce
Salt and pepper to taste
1   loaf (1 pound) frozen bread dough, thawed
1   cup (4 ounces) shredded cheddar cheese

In a skillet, cook beef over medium heat until no longer pink; drain. Stir in the cream of mushroom soup, mushrooms, onion, Worcestershire sauce, salt and pepper. Remove from the heat.

On a floured surface, roll the bread dough into a 16-in. x 8-in. rectangle. Carefully cut the dough into eight squares.

Place about 1/3 cup of the meat mixture in the center of each square; sprinkle meat mixture with shredded cheddar cheese. Bring the four corners to center over the filling; pinch the seams together to seal.

Place seam side down on greased baking sheets. Cover and let rise in a warm place for 15-20 minutes. Bake at 350° for 20-25 minutes or until golden brown. YIELD: 8 SERVINGS.

Swedish Meatballs

SHERYL LUDEMAN • KENOSHA, WISCONSIN

This recipe relies on ingredients we always have on hand and doesn't dirty many dishes. While the tender meatballs cook in the microwave, boil the noodles on the stovetop to get this saucy entree on the table in minutes.

PREP/TOTAL TIME: 30 min.

1   small onion, chopped
1   egg
1/4   cup seasoned bread crumbs
2   tablespoons milk
1/2   teaspoon salt
1/8   teaspoon pepper
1   pound ground beef

SAUCE:
1   can (10-3/4 ounces) condensed cream of mushroom soup, undiluted
1/2   cup sour cream
1/4   cup milk
1   tablespoon dried parsley flakes
1/4   teaspoon ground nutmeg, optional
Hot cooked noodles

In a bowl, combine the onion, egg, bread crumbs, milk, salt and pepper. Add beef; mix well. Shape into 1-in. meatballs, about 24. Place meatballs in a shallow 1-1/2-qt. microwave-safe dish. Cover and microwave on high or 7-1/2 minutes or until meat is no longer pink; drain.

Combine the soup, sour cream, milk, parsley and nutmeg if desired; pour over meatballs. Cover and cook on high for 5-6 minutes or until heated through. Serve over noodles. YIELD: 4 SERVINGS.

EDITOR'S NOTE: This recipe was tested in a 1,100-watt microwave.

swedish meatballs

Simple Mushroom Stew

CHERIE SECHRIST • RED LION, PENNSYLVANIA

Even with chunky vegetables and tender stew meat, the mushrooms star in this stick-to-your-ribs main dish. I got the recipe from my cousin and adapted it for my mushroom-loving family who just loves it.

PREP: 10 min. **BAKE:** 2-1/2 hours

1	can (10-3/4 ounces) condensed tomato soup, undiluted
1	can (10-3/4 ounces) condensed cream of mushroom soup, undiluted
2-1/2	cups water
2	pounds beef stew meat, cut into cubes
2	bay leaves
3	medium potatoes, peeled and cut into 1-inch chunks
4	carrots, cut into 1/2-inch slices
1	pound medium fresh mushrooms, halved
1	tablespoon quick-cooking tapioca

In a Dutch oven, stir the soups and water until smooth. Add meat and bay leaves. Cover and bake at 325° for 1-1/2 hours.

Stir in potatoes, carrots, mushrooms and tapioca. Cover and bake 1 hour longer or until the meat and vegetables are tender. Discard the bay leaves before serving. YIELD: 6-8 SERVINGS.

simple mushroom stew

Saucy Beef Casserole

FERNE SPIELVOGEL • FAIRWATER, WISCONSIN

I rely on canned soups and crunchy chow mein noodles to flavor this hearty ground beef bake.

PREP: 10 min. **BAKE:** 30 min.

1	pound ground beef
1	medium onion, chopped
1	can (10-3/4 ounces) condensed cream of chicken soup, undiluted
1	can (10-3/4 ounces) condensed vegetable soup, undiluted
3/4	cup chow mein noodles

In a skillet, cook beef and onion over medium heat until meat is no longer pink; drain. Stir in soups. Transfer to a greased 8-in. square baking dish.

Cover and bake at 350° for 25-30 minutes or until heated through. Uncover; sprinkle with chow mein noodles. Bake 5 minutes longer or until chow mein noodles are crisp. YIELD: 4 SERVINGS.

Sauerkraut Hot Dish

LUCY MOHLMAN • CRETE, NEBRASKA

This tasty creation was brought to a school picnic by a neighbor. Needless to say, she took home an empty pan—and we all took home the recipe.

PREP: 15 min. **BAKE:** 45 min.

1	pound ground beef
1/4	cup chopped onion
1/2	teaspoon salt
1/2	teaspoon pepper
1	can (32 ounces) sauerkraut, rinsed and well drained
2	cups uncooked egg noodles
1	can (10-3/4 ounces) condensed cream of celery soup, undiluted
1	can (10-3/4 ounces) condensed cream of mushroom soup, undiluted
1	cup milk
1	to 1-1/2 cups (4 to 6 ounces) shredded cheddar cheese

In a skillet, brown ground beef, onion, salt and pepper; drain. Spoon half of the ground beef mixture into a 13-in. x 9-in. x 2-in. baking dish. Top with half of the sauerkraut and half of the noodles. Repeat layers. Combine soups and milk; pour over noodles.

Cover and bake at 350° for 30 minutes. Remove from oven and sprinkle with cheese; return to oven for 15 to 20 minutes. YIELD: 4-6 SERVINGS.

Bacon Nut Meatballs

SUE DOWNES-WILLIAMS • LEBANON, NEW HAMPSHIRE

Almonds provide the crunchy difference in these irresistible meatballs. Making them a day in advance is convenient and enhances the flavor even more.

PREP: 25 min. **COOK:** 30 min.

10	bacon strips, diced
2	eggs
1/3	cup tomato paste
1-1/2	cups soft bread crumbs
1/3	cup minced fresh parsley
2	tablespoons chopped slivered almonds
1	tablespoon dried oregano
1	tablespoon salt
1-1/2	teaspoons pepper
2	pounds ground beef
1	pound fresh mushrooms, sliced
1	medium onion, chopped
2	cans (10-3/4 ounces *each*) condensed cream of mushroom soup, undiluted
1	can (10-1/2 ounces) beef consomme

In a large skillet, cook bacon. Remove bacon with a slotted spoon; drain on paper towels. Reserve the drippings in skillet.

In a large bowl, combine the eggs, tomato paste, bread crumbs, parsley, almonds, oregano, salt, pepper and bacon. Crumble beef over mixture and mix well.

Shape into 1-in. balls. Brown meatballs in drippings. Remove with a slotted spoon. Drain, reserving 1 tablespoon drippings. Saute mushrooms and onion in the drippings.

Combine soup and consomme; stir into the mushroom mixture until blended. Return meatballs to pan. Bring to a boil; reduce heat. Simmer, uncovered, for 10 minutes or until meat is no longer pink.
YIELD: 60 MEATBALLS.

cooking tip

Here's a hint to make meatballs the same size. First, lightly pat the meat mixture into a 1-in.-thick rectangle. Then cut the rectangle into the same number of squares as meatballs in the recipe. Roll each square into a ball and you're done!

black-eyed pea casserole

Black-Eyed Pea Casserole

KATHY ROGERS • NATCHEZ, MISSISSIPPI

This group-size dish is quick, simple and delicious. People always ask for "just a little more." I guess you could call it one of my Southern favorites.

PREP: 20 min. **BAKE:** 20 min.

2	packages (6 ounces *each*) long grain and wild rice mix
2	pounds ground beef
2	medium onions, chopped
2	small green peppers, chopped
4	cans (15-1/2 ounces *each*) black-eyed peas with jalapenos, rinsed and drained
2	cans (10-3/4 ounces *each*) condensed cream of mushroom soup, undiluted
1-1/3	cups shredded cheddar cheese

In a large saucepan, cook the rice mixes according to package directions. Meanwhile, in a large skillet, cook the beef, onions and green peppers over medium heat until the meat is no longer pink; drain.

In a large bowl, combine the black-eyed peas, soup, rice and beef mixture. Transfer to two greased 2-1/2-qt. baking dishes.

Cover and bake at 350° for 20-25 minutes or until heated through. Uncover; sprinkle with cheese. Bake 5 minutes longer or until cheese is melted. YIELD: 2 CASSEROLES (10-12 SERVINGS EACH).

flavorful beef in gravy

Flavorful Beef in Gravy

CHERYL SINDERGARD • PLOVER, IOWA

Served over noodles, this home-style supper showcases tender chunks of savory beef stew meat. I use canned soups and onion soup mix to make the easy, mouth-watering gravy. With a green salad and a loaf of crusty bread, dinner is complete.

PREP: 15 min. **COOK:** 7 hours

1/3	cup all-purpose flour
3	pounds beef stew meat, cut into 1-inch cubes
3	tablespoons vegetable oil
2	cans (10-3/4 ounces *each*) condensed cream of mushroom soup, undiluted
1	can (10-3/4 ounces) condensed golden mushroom soup, undiluted
1	can (10-3/4 ounces) condensed cream of celery soup, undiluted
1-1/3	cups milk
1	envelope onion soup mix

Hot cooked noodles *or* mashed potatoes

Place flour in a large resealable plastic bag; add beef and toss to coat. In a skillet, brown beef in oil. Transfer beef to a 5-qt. slow cooker. Stir in the soups, milk and soup mix. Cover and cook on low for 7-8 hours or until the meat is tender. Serve over noodles or potatoes. YIELD: 10-12 SERVINGS.

Sauerkraut-Beef Bake

DOLORES SKROUT • SUMMERHILL, PENNSYLVANIA

My husband goes to school and works full-time, and I am the mother of a 1-year old. With a busy schedule like ours, this quick meal-in-one that relies on pantry staples is a real time-saver!

PREP: 15 min. **BAKE:** 1 hour

1	pound ground beef
1	can (27 ounces) sauerkraut, rinsed and well drained
1/2	cup uncooked instant rice
1	can (10-3/4 ounces) condensed cream of mushroom soup, undiluted
1	soup can water
1/2	package dry onion soup mix
1	can (4 ounces) mushroom stems and pieces, drained, optional

In a skillet, cook beef over medium heat until no longer pink. Drain.

In a greased 2-quart casserole, combine beef with sauerkraut, rice, soup, water and soup mix. Add mushrooms if desired. Cover and bake at 350° for 1 hour. YIELD: 6 SERVINGS.

Cheesy Beef Macaroni

DENA EVETTS • SENTINEL, OKLAHOMA

Little ones will light up the room with smiles when you bring this five-ingredient pleaser to the table. Crunchy canned corn is an appealing addition to the mild and cheesy combination of ground beef and pasta.

PREP: 25 min. **BAKE:** 20 min.

1	pound ground beef
1	can (15-1/4 ounces) whole kernel corn, drained
1	can (10-3/4 ounces) condensed cream of chicken soup, undiluted
8	ounces process cheese (Velveeta), shredded
2-1/2	cups cooked elbow macaroni

In a large skillet, cook beef over medium heat until no longer pink; drain. Add the corn and soup. Set aside 1/2 cup cheese for topping; stir remaining cheese into meat mixture until melted. Gently stir in macaroni until coated.

Transfer to a greased 8-in. square baking dish. Top with the reserved cheese. Bake, uncovered, at 350° for 20-25 minutes or until it is heated through. YIELD: 4-6 SERVINGS.

Beef & Broccoli Casserole

DOROTHY BUTTRILL • FAIRFIELD, TEXAS

I came up with this recipe on one of those "what in the world can I fix for dinner" days. I usually have all the ingredients on hand, so it is a handy dish when I need to fix something in a hurry. I'm sure it will become a weeknight favorite with your family, too.

PREP: 20 min. **BAKE:** 15 min.

- 1   pound ground beef
- 1/2   cup chopped onion
- 1   tablespoon olive oil
- 1   tablespoon Worcestershire sauce
- 1   teaspoon garlic salt
- 1   teaspoon Italian seasoning
- 1   cup uncooked instant rice
- 1   can (10-3/4 ounces) condensed cream of mushroom soup, undiluted
- 1/2   cup water
- 2   pounds fresh broccoli, chopped *or* 6 cups frozen chopped broccoli, cooked and drained
- 6   ounces sliced part-skim mozzarella cheese

Chopped fresh parsley, optional

In a skillet, cook beef and onion in oil until beef is no longer pink and onion is tender; drain. Combine beef with Worcestershire sauce, garlic salt, Italian seasoning, rice, soup and water.

Place cooked broccoli in an 11-in. x 7-in. x 2-in. baking dish; spoon meat mixture over. Top with mozzarella cheese. Bake, uncovered, at 400° for 15 to 20 minutes. Garnish with parsley if desired. YIELD: 6 SERVINGS.

Swiss Steak With Dumplings

PAT HABIGER • SPEARVILLE, KANSAS

My mother was a great cook and I learned so much from her. Years ago, I entered this down-home recipe in a contest and won. While it's a comforting choice during cooler weather, it's a favorite all year long.

PREP: 25 min. **BAKE:** 70 min.

- 2   pounds boneless beef top loin steaks (about 3/4 inch), trimmed
- 1/3   cup all-purpose flour
- 2   tablespoons vegetable oil
- 2   cans (10-3/4 ounces *each*) condensed cream of chicken soup, undiluted
- 1-1/3 cups water
- 1/2   teaspoon salt
- 1/8   teaspoon pepper

DUMPLINGS:
- 1/2   cup dry bread crumbs
- 5   tablespoons butter, melted, *divided*
- 1-1/3 cups all-purpose flour
- 2   teaspoons baking powder
- 1/2   teaspoon salt
- 1/4   teaspoon poultry seasoning
- 2/3   cup milk

Cut steaks into six or eight pieces; dredge in flour. In a large skillet, brown meat in oil on both sides. Transfer to a greased 2-1/2-qt. baking dish.

In the same skillet, combine the soup, water, salt and pepper; bring to a boil, stirring occasionally. Pour over steak. Cover and bake at 350° for 50-60 minutes or until meat is tender.

For dumplings, combine the bread crumbs and 2 tablespoons butter in a small bowl; set aside. In another bowl, combine the flour, baking powder, salt and poultry seasoning. Stir in milk and remaining butter just until moistened.

Drop by rounded tablespoonfuls into the crumb mixture; roll until coated. Place dumplings over steak. Bake, uncovered, at 425° for 20-30 minutes or until dumplings are lightly browned and a toothpick inserted in a dumpling comes out clean. YIELD: 6-8 SERVINGS.

swiss steak with dumplings

Veggie Meatball Medley

BARBARA KERNOHAN • FOREST, ONTARIO

I developed this recipe in an attempt to offer a simple, well-balanced meal the whole family would enjoy. Everyone raves about the soy-flavored sauce.

PREP: 15 min. **COOK:** 20 min.

1	egg
1/4	cup dry bread crumbs
1/2	teaspoon salt
1/4	teaspoon pepper
1	pound ground beef
2	cups frozen stir-fry vegetable blend
1	medium onion, chopped
1	can (10-3/4 ounces) condensed cream of mushroom soup, undiluted
1/4	cup soy sauce
1/4	teaspoon garlic powder

Hot cooked rice

In a large bowl, combine the first four ingredients. Crumble beef over mixture and mix well. Shape into 1-1/2-in. balls. In a large nonstick skillet, cook meatballs, vegetables and onion until the meatballs are browned; drain.

Stir in the soup, soy sauce and garlic powder. Bring to a boil. Reduce heat; simmer, uncovered, for 20 minutes or until the meat is no longer pink, stirring occasionally. Serve over rice. YIELD: 4 SERVINGS.

tortilla beef bake

Tortilla Beef Bake

KIM OSBURN • LIGONIER, INDIANA

My family loves Mexican food, so I came up with this no-fuss entree that gets its spark from a jar of store-bought salsa. We like this satisfying dish so much that there are rarely any leftovers.

PREP: 10 min. **BAKE:** 30 min.

1-1/2	pounds ground beef
1	can (10-3/4 ounces) condensed cream of chicken soup, undiluted
2-1/2	cups crushed tortilla chips, *divided*
1	jar (16 ounces) salsa
1-1/2	cups (6 ounces) shredded cheddar cheese

In a skillet, cook beef over medium heat until no longer pink; drain. Stir in soup. Sprinkle 1-1/2 cups tortilla chips in a greased shallow 2-1/2-qt. baking dish. Top with beef mixture, salsa and cheese.

veggie meatball medley

cooking tip

For added zip in Tortilla Beef Bake, use medium or hot salsa, depending on your family's taste. For both Tortilla Beef Bake and Mexican Chip Casserole, give the dishes even more kick by replacing the listed cheese with pepper Jack cheese.

Bake, uncovered, at 350° for 25-30 minutes or until bubbly. Sprinkle with the remaining chips. Bake 3 minutes longer or until chips are lightly toasted. YIELD: 6 SERVINGS.

Beefy Spinach Noodle Bake

PRISCILLA GILBERT • INDIAN HARBOUR BEACH, FLORIDA

I enjoy trying new, uncomplicated recipes, and when I find a winner like this, I'm eager to share it with many. I round out the supper by serving steamed buttered carrots and fresh-from-the-oven rolls.

PREP: 25 min. BAKE: 40 min.

1	pound ground beef
1	small onion, chopped
4-3/4	cups uncooked wide egg noodles
1	can (10-3/4 ounces) condensed cream of mushroom soup, undiluted
3/4	cup milk

SPINACH LAYER:

3	tablespoons butter
2	tablespoons all-purpose flour
1/2	teaspoon paprika
1/2	teaspoon salt
1/4	teaspoon pepper
1/8	teaspoon ground nutmeg
1	cup milk
2	packages (10 ounces *each*) frozen chopped spinach, thawed and squeezed dry
1/4	cup thinly sliced green onions
2	cups (8 ounces) shredded Swiss cheese, *divided*
2/3	cup crushed French-fried onions

In a skillet, cook beef and onion over medium heat until meat is no longer pink; drain. Cook noodles according to package directions; drain. In a large bowl, combine soup and milk until blended. Stir in beef mixture and noodles; set aside.

For spinach layer, in a large saucepan, melt butter. Whisk in flour, paprika, salt, pepper and nutmeg until smooth. Gradually whisk in milk. Bring to a boil; cook and stir for 1-2 minutes or until thickened. Stir in spinach and green onions.

In a greased shallow 2-1/2-qt. baking dish, layer half of the beef mixture and half of the cheese. Top with spinach mixture and remaining beef mixture. Cover and bake at 375° for 35 minutes. Uncover; sprinkle with remaining cheese. Top with French-fried onions. Bake 5-10 minutes longer or until cheese is melted. YIELD: 6-8 SERVINGS.

mexican chip casserole

Mexican Chip Casserole

DORIS HEATH • FRANKLIN, NORTH CAROLINA

This pleasing, one-dish dinner relies on convenient packaged ingredients to create an entree with spoonfuls of Southwestern flair. There is nothing tricky about the preparation, and I have plenty of time to set the table while it bakes in the oven.

PREP/TOTAL TIME: 20 min.

1	pound ground beef
1	medium onion, chopped
1	garlic clove, minced
1	can (10-3/4 ounces) condensed cream of mushroom soup, undiluted
1	can (11 ounces) Mexicorn
1	can (4 ounces) chopped green chilies
1	package (10-1/2 ounces) corn chips
1	can (10 ounces) enchilada sauce
1	to 2 cups (4 to 8 ounces) shredded Colby-Monterey Jack cheese

In a skillet, cook beef, onion and garlic over medium heat until meat is no longer pink and onion is tender; drain. Add soup, corn and chilies; mix well.

In an ungreased shallow 3-qt. baking dish, layer meat mixture, chips and sauce; top with cheese. Bake, uncovered, at 350° for 8-10 minutes or until heated through. YIELD: 6 SERVINGS.

country goulash skillet

Round Steak Supper

SANDRA CASTILLO • JANESVILLE, WISCONSIN

Here's a meat-and-potatoes dinner that will help you stick to your budget. Inexpensive round steak and potatoes are simmered for hours in an onion-flavored gravy to create this satisfying supper.

PREP: 10 min. **COOK:** 6 hours

4	large potatoes, peeled and cut into 1/2-inch cubes
1-1/2	pounds boneless beef round steak
1	can (10-3/4 ounces) condensed cream of mushroom soup, undiluted
1/2	cup water
1	envelope onion soup mix

Pepper and garlic powder to taste

Place the potatoes in a 3-qt. slow cooker. Cut beef into four pieces; place over potatoes.

In a bowl, combine the soup, water, soup mix, pepper and garlic powder. Pour over the beef. Cover and cook on low for 6-8 hours or until meat and potatoes are tender. YIELD: 4 SERVINGS.

Country Goulash Skillet

LISA NEUBERT • SOUTH OGDEN, UTAH

I have found that basic recipes like this never go out of style. My homegrown vegetables, including onions, peppers and corn make every bite extra-special.

PREP: 15 min. **COOK:** 20 min.

1	pound ground beef
1	can (28 ounces) stewed tomatoes
1	can (10-3/4 ounces) condensed cream of mushroom soup, undiluted
2	cups fresh *or* frozen corn
1	medium green pepper, chopped
1	medium onion, chopped
1	tablespoon Worcestershire sauce
3	cups cooked elbow macaroni

In a large skillet, cook beef over medium heat until no longer pink; drain. Stir in the tomatoes, soup, corn, green pepper, onion and Worcestershire sauce. Bring to a boil. Reduce heat; cover and simmer for 20-25 minutes or until vegetables are tender. Stir in macaroni and heat through. YIELD: 6-8 SERVINGS.

Hamburger 'n' Fries Dinner

SHELLY RYUN • MALVERN, IOWA

I got the idea for this casserole from our church cookbook. I played with the ingredients until it was just the way my family likes it. The combination of ground beef, French fries and cheese is always a hit...especially when served like this!

PREP: 20 min. **BAKE:** 30 min.

1	pound ground beef
1	small onion, chopped
2	cups frozen French fries, thawed
1	can (15-1/4 ounces) whole kernel corn, drained
1	can (10-3/4 ounces) condensed cream of mushroom soup, undiluted
1/2	cup shredded process American cheese (Velveeta)

In a skillet, cook beef and onion over medium heat until the meat is no longer pink; drain. Line a greased 9-in. square baking dish with French fries. Top with beef mixture, corn, soup and cheese. Bake, uncovered, at 375° for 30 minutes or until hot and bubbly. YIELD: 4-6 SERVINGS.

Creamy Beef With Biscuits

MARY MILLER • SHREVE, OHIO

With 11 children, my mom had lots of cooking experience. She generously passed down her knowledge and recipes. Mom usually served this dish to company.

PREP: 10 min. **BAKE:** 35 min.

2	pounds ground beef
1	medium onion, chopped
1	package (8 ounces) cream cheese, cubed
1	can (10-3/4 ounces) condensed cream of mushroom soup, undiluted
3/4	cup milk
1/2	cup ketchup
1/2	teaspoon salt
1/4	teaspoon pepper
1	tube (12 ounces) refrigerated buttermilk biscuits

In a large skillet, cook beef and onion over medium heat until meat is no longer pink; drain. Add cream cheese, stirring until melted. Add the soup, milk, ketchup, salt and pepper; mix well.

Transfer to a greased 13-in. x 9-in. x 2-in. baking dish. Cover and bake at 375° for 15 minutes. Uncover; arrange the biscuits over top. Bake 20-25 minutes longer or until the biscuits are golden brown. YIELD: 8-10 SERVINGS.

cooking tip

When purchasing ground beef, you want to look for meat that is bright red in color and is in a tightly sealed package. Be sure to buy ground beef before the "sell-by" date that is posted on the the package. When using it in recipes, keep in mind that 1 pound of ground beef serves 3 to 4 people.

Steak Roll-Ups

PAT HABIGER • SPEARVILLE, KANSAS

My family tells me these hearty stuffed beef rolls with creamy sauce "taste like home." They are attractive enough to serve for a special dinner but economical and easy to prepare for everyday meals.

PREP: 20 min. **COOK:** 2 hours

1-1/2	pounds boneless beef round steak
1/4	cup chopped onion
1/4	cup butter, melted
2	cups fresh bread cubes
1/2	cup chopped celery
1	tablespoon dried parsley flakes
1/2	teaspoon salt
1/2	teaspoon poultry seasoning
1/4	teaspoon pepper
1	cup all-purpose flour
2	tablespoons vegetable oil
1	can (10-3/4 ounces) condensed cream of mushroom soup, undiluted
1-1/3	cups water
3/4	teaspoon browning sauce, optional

Pound steak to 1/3-in. thickness. Cut into six pieces. Combine the next eight ingredients; mix well. Place 1/3 cup on each piece of steak; roll up and fasten with a toothpick. Roll in flour.

In a large skillet, brown roll-ups in oil. Combine soup, water and browning sauce if desired; pour over roll-ups. Cover and simmer for 2 hours or until meat is tender, turning occasionally. YIELD: 6 SERVINGS.

steak roll-ups

Round Steak
With Dumplings

SHERRI ODOM • PLANT CITY, FLORIDA

My grandmother taught me how to make this comforting dish. I like to serve it for special occasions.

PREP: 30 min. **BAKE:** 1 hour 50 min.

3/4	cup all-purpose flour
1	tablespoon paprika
3	pounds boneless beef top round steak, cut into serving-size pieces
2	to 3 tablespoons vegetable oil
1	medium onion, chopped
2-2/3	cups water
2	cans (10-3/4 ounces *each)* condensed cream of chicken soup, undiluted
1/2	teaspoon pepper

DUMPLINGS:

3	cups all-purpose flour
1/4	cup dried minced onion
2	tablespoons baking powder
1	tablespoon poppy seeds
1-1/2	teaspoons celery salt
1-1/2	teaspoons poultry seasoning
3/4	teaspoon salt
1-1/2	cups milk
6	tablespoons vegetable oil
1	cup dry bread crumbs
1/4	cup butter, melted

In a large resealable plastic bag, combine flour and paprika. Add beef, a few pieces at a time, and shake to coat.

In a Dutch oven over medium-high heat, brown steak in oil on both sides in batches, adding more oil if necessary. Remove and keep warm.

In the drippings, saute the onion until tender. Stir in the water, soup and pepper. Bring to a boil.

round steak with dumplings

Return the meat to pan. Cover and bake at 325° for 1-1/2 hours.

Meanwhile, for dumplings, combine the flour, onion, baking powder, poppy seeds, celery salt, poultry seasoning and salt. Combine milk and oil; stir into dry ingredients just until moistened.

Increase oven temperature to 425°. In a large bowl, combine bread crumbs and butter. Drop dumpling batter by rounded tablespoonfuls into crumb mixture; roll to form dumplings. Place on top of simmering beef mixture.

Cover and bake 20-25 minutes longer or until a toothpick inserted in a dumpling comes out clean (do not lift the cover while baking). YIELD: 10-12 SERVINGS.

Enchilada Casserole

DENISE WALLER • OMAHA, NEBRASKA

Tortilla chips and a side salad turn this casserole into a mouth-watering meal. Besides its wonderful flavor, I love that this hearty main dish comes together with only a handful of ingredients and cooks in my slow cooker. It couldn't get any easier!

PREP: 20 min. **COOK:** 6 hours

1	pound ground beef
2	cans (10 ounces *each)* enchilada sauce
1	can (10-3/4 ounces) condensed cream of onion soup, undiluted
1/4	teaspoon salt
1	package (8-1/2 ounces) flour tortillas, torn
3	cups (12 ounces) shredded cheddar cheese

In a skillet, cook beef over medium heat until no longer pink; drain. Stir in the enchilada sauce, soup and salt.

In a 3-qt. slow cooker, layer a third of the beef mixture, tortillas and cheese. Repeat the layers twice. Cover and cook on low for 6-8 hours or until heated through. YIELD: 4 SERVINGS.

Potluck Hot Dish

DOROTHY FRIEZ • MCLAUGHLIN, SOUTH DAKOTA

This beef and pork combination is my favorite item to take to bring-a-dish dinners. The down-home ingredients make it a guaranteed crowd-pleaser. The recipe is often requested, and I never hesitate to share it.

PREP: 15 min. **BAKE:** 1 hour

1	pound ground pork
1	pound ground beef

1   large onion, chopped
1   medium green pepper, chopped
1   package (7 ounces) elbow *or* ring
      macaroni, cooked and drained
2   cans (14-3/4 ounces *each*) cream-style
      corn
2   cans (11-1/2 ounces *each*) condensed
      chicken with rice soup, undiluted
1   can (10-3/4 ounces) condensed cream
      of mushroom soup, undiluted
1   teaspoon salt
1/2   teaspoon pepper
Seasoned salt to taste
1/2   cup dry bread crumbs
2   tablespoons butter, melted

In a large skillet, cook the meat, onion and green pepper over medium heat until meat is no longer pink; drain. Stir in macaroni, corn, soups and seasonings.

Transfer to a greased 13-in. x 9-in. x 2-in. baking dish. Toss bread crumbs and butter; sprinkle over top. Cover and bake at 350° for 45 minutes. Uncover and bake for 15 minutes longer or until heated through. YIELD: 12 SERVINGS.

Beefy
Au Gratin Potatoes

EILEEN MAJERUS • PINE ISLAND, MINNESOTA

Vary the flavor of this family-favorite casserole by using different kinds of soup and potato mixes. I usually serve hearty helpings with a crisp garden salad and a loaf of freshly baked garlic bread.

PREP: 20 min. **COOK:** 4 hours

1   package (5-1/4 ounces) au gratin
      potatoes *or* cheddar and bacon
      potatoes
1   can (15-1/4 ounces) whole kernel corn,
      drained
1   can (10-3/4 ounces) condensed cream
      of potato soup, undiluted
1   cup water
1   can (4 ounces) chopped green chilies,
      drained
1   can (4 ounces) mushroom stems and
      pieces, drained
1   jar (4 ounces) diced pimientos, drained
1   pound ground beef
1   medium onion, chopped

Set the potato sauce mix aside. Place potatoes in a 3-qt. slow cooker; top with corn. In a bowl, combine soup, water, chilies, mushrooms, pimientos and reserved sauce mix; mix well. Pour a third of the

tater-topped casserole

mixture over corn. In a skillet, cook beef and onion over medium heat until the meat is no longer pink; drain. Transfer to slow cooker. Top with remaining sauce mixture. Do not stir. Cover and cook on low for 4 hours or until potatoes are tender. YIELD: 4-6 SERVINGS.

Tater-Topped Casserole

VICTORIA MITCHELL • SALEM, VIRGINIA

I grew up enjoying this cheesy potato bake. My mom always saw smiles around the table whenever she served it. I'm certain you'll get the same results.

PREP: 15 min. **BAKE:** 45 min.

1/2   cup chopped onion
1/3   cup sliced celery
1   pound lean ground beef
1/2   teaspoon salt
1/4   teaspoon pepper
1   can (10-3/4 ounces) condensed cream
      of celery soup, undiluted
1   package (16 ounces) frozen Tater Tots
1   cup (4 ounces) shredded cheddar
      cheese

In a skillet, cook onion, celery and ground beef until the meat is no longer pink and the vegetables are tender. Drain. Stir in salt and pepper.

Spoon mixture into a greased 12-in. x 8-in. x 2-in. baking dish. Spread soup over meat mixture. Top with frozen potatoes. Bake at 400° for about 40 minutes or until bubbly. Remove from oven and sprinkle with cheese. Return to oven and bake 5 minutes longer or until cheese melted. YIELD: 4-6 SERVINGS.

mashed potato hot dish

Mashed Potato Hot Dish

TANYA ABERNATHY • YACOLT, WASHINGTON

My cousin gave me this simple but mouth-watering recipe. Whenever I'm making homemade mashed potatoes, I throw in a few extra spuds so I can make this dish for supper the following night.

PREP: 15 min. **BAKE:** 20 min.

1	pound ground beef
1	can (10-3/4 ounces) condensed cream of chicken soup, undiluted
2	cups frozen French-style green beans
2	cups hot mashed potatoes (prepared with milk and butter)
1/2	cup shredded cheddar cheese

In a large skillet, cook beef over medium heat until no longer pink; drain. Stir in soup and beans.

Transfer to a greased 2-qt. baking dish. Top with mashed potatoes; sprinkle with cheese.

Bake, uncovered, at 350° for 20-25 minutes or until bubbly and cheese is melted. YIELD: 4 SERVINGS.

cooking tip

About 1-1/4 pounds of potatoes will yield a generous 2 cups mashed potatoes...just the right amount for scrumptious Mashed Potato Hot Dish.

Asparagus Shepherd's Pie

STEVE ROWLAND • FREDERICKSBURG, VIRGINIA

This version of Shepherd's Pie takes a tasty twist. Between the fluffy mashed potato topping and the savory ground beef base is a bed of tender, green asparagus. Even my kids ask for big helpings.

PREP: 25 min. **BAKE:** 20 min.

6	medium potatoes, peeled and quartered
1	pound ground beef
1	large onion, chopped
2	garlic cloves, minced
1	can (10-3/4 ounces) condensed cream of asparagus soup, undiluted
1/4	teaspoon pepper
1	pound fresh asparagus, trimmed and cut into 1-inch pieces
1/2	cup milk
1/4	cup butter
1	teaspoon rubbed sage
3/4	teaspoon salt
1/2	cup shredded part-skim mozzarella cheese

Paprika

In a saucepan, cover potatoes with water; cook until very tender. Meanwhile, in a skillet, cook beef, onion and garlic over medium heat until meat is no longer pink; drain. Stir in soup and pepper; pour into a greased 2-qt. baking dish.

Cook asparagus in a small amount of water until crisp-tender, about 3-4 minutes; drain and place over beef mixture.

Drain potatoes; mash with milk, butter, sage and salt. Spread over the asparagus. Sprinkle with cheese and paprika. Bake, uncovered, at 350° for 20 minutes. YIELD: 6-8 SERVINGS.

Roast Beef & Gravy

ABBY METZGER • LARCHWOOD, IOWA

This is by far the easiest way to make roast beef and gravy. On busy days, I can put this main dish in the slow cooker and forget about it. My family likes it with mashed potatoes and fruit salad.

PREP: 15 min. **COOK:** 8 hours

1	boneless beef chuck roast (3 pounds)
2	cans (10-3/4 ounces *each*) condensed cream of mushroom soup, undiluted

simple salisbury steak

1/3   cup sherry *or* beef broth
1   envelope onion soup mix

Cut roast in half; place in a 3-qt. slow cooker. In a large bowl, combine the remaining ingredients; pour over roast. Cover and cook on low for 8-9 hours or until meat is tender. YIELD: 8-10 SERVINGS.

Simple Salisbury Steak

ELOUISE BONAR • HANOVER, ILLINOIS

Fresh mushrooms and a can of cream of mushroom soup create the speedy, simmered sauce that covers these moist ground beef patties. The family-pleasing entree is perfect for during the week.

PREP/TOTAL TIME: 30 min.

1   egg
1/3   cup dry bread crumbs
1   can (10-3/4 ounces) condensed cream of mushroom soup, undiluted, *divided*
1/4   cup finely chopped onion
1   pound ground beef
1/2   cup milk
1/4   teaspoon browning sauce, optional
1/4   teaspoon salt
1-1/2   cups sliced fresh mushrooms

In a bowl, combine the egg, bread crumbs, 1/4 cup soup and onion. Crumble the beef over mixture and mix well. Shape into six patties. In a large nonstick skillet, brown the patties on both sides; drain.

In a bowl, combine the milk, browning sauce if desired, salt and remaining soup; stir in mushrooms. Pour over patties. Reduce heat; cover and simmer for 15-20 minutes or until meat is no longer pink. YIELD: 6 SERVINGS.

Save-a-Penny Casserole

JANICE MILLER • WORTHINGTON, KENTUCKY

At the office where I worked years ago, we women often shared our favorite recipes at lunchtime. This casserole came from a co-worker, and my family has enjoyed it for some 30 years. Besides being quick to prepare, it is very economical.

PREP: 10 min. **BAKE:** 30 min.

1   pound ground beef
1   can (10-3/4 ounces) condensed cream of mushroom soup, undiluted
1   can (14-3/4 ounces) spaghetti in tomato sauce with cheese
1   can (15 to 16 ounces) mixed vegetables, drained
1   cups (4 ounces) shredded cheddar cheese, optional

In a skillet, brown beef; drain. Stir in the soup, spaghetti and vegetables. Transfer to an ungreased 11-in. x 7-in. x 2-in. baking dish.

Bake, uncovered, at 350° for 30 minutes or until heated through. If desired, sprinkle with the cheddar cheese and let casserole stand a few minutes until melted. YIELD: 4-6 SERVINGS.

save-a-penny casserole

Lazy Pierogi Bake

SANDY STARKS • AMHERST, NEW YORK

A favorite dish in our family is pierogi—tasty pockets of dough filled with cottage cheese and onions. Making it is time-consuming, so my mom came up with this easy casserole that is filled with rich pierogi flavor without all the effort.

PREP: 25 min. **BAKE:** 35 min.

1	package (16 ounces) spiral pasta
1	pound sliced bacon, diced
2	medium onions, chopped
2	garlic cloves, minced
1/2	pound fresh mushrooms, sliced
2	cans (14 ounces *each*) sauerkraut, rinsed and well drained
3	cans (10-3/4 ounces *each*) condensed cream of mushroom soup, undiluted
1/2	cup milk
1/2	teaspoon celery seed
1/8	teaspoon pepper

Cook pasta according to package directions. Meanwhile, in a skillet, cook bacon over medium heat until crisp. Remove the bacon to paper towels; drain, reserving 2 tablespoons drippings.

In the drippings, saute onions and garlic until tender. Add the mushrooms; cook until tender. Stir in the sauerkraut and half of the bacon. In a bowl, combine the soup, milk, celery seed and pepper. Drain pasta.

Place a fourth of the pasta in two greased 13-in. x 9-in. x 2-in. baking dishes. Top each with a fourth of the sauerkraut and soup mixture. Repeat layers.

Cover and bake at 350° for 25 minutes. Uncover; sprinkle with remaining bacon. Bake 10-15 minutes longer or until heated through. Let stand for 5-10 minutes before serving. YIELD: 16 SERVINGS.

cooking tip

For added convenience, purchase packages of cubed deli ham for recipes like Veggie Noodle Ham Casserole and others that call for fully cooked ham. Available near the lunch meats, the packages help you get dinner on the table fast!

veggie noodle ham casserole

Veggie Noodle Ham Casserole

JUDY MOODY • WHEATLEY, ONTARIO

This saucy main course is quite versatile. Without the ham, it can be a vegetarian entree or a hearty side dish.

PREP: 15 min. **BAKE:** 50 min.

1	package (12 ounces) wide egg noodles
1	can (10-3/4 ounces) condensed cream of chicken soup, undiluted
1	can (10-3/4 ounces) condensed cream of broccoli soup, undiluted
1-1/2	cups milk
2	cups frozen corn, thawed
1-1/2	cups frozen California-blend vegetables, thawed
1-1/2	cups cubed fully cooked ham
2	tablespoons minced fresh parsley
1/2	teaspoon pepper
1/4	teaspoon salt
1	cup (4 ounces) shredded cheddar cheese, *divided*

Cook pasta according to package directions; drain. In a large bowl, combine soups and milk; stir in the noodles, corn, vegetables, ham, parsley, pepper, salt and 3/4 cup of cheese.

Transfer to a greased 13-in. x 9-in. x 2-in. baking dish. Cover and bake at 350° for 45 minutes. Uncover; sprinkle with remaining cheese. Bake for 5-10 minutes longer or until bubbly and the cheese is melted. YIELD: 8-10 SERVINGS.

slow-cooked ham 'n' broccoli

Oven-Baked Chop Suey

NADINE DAHLING • ELKADER, IOWA

Whenever I take this casserole to a potluck, I come home with an empty dish and several requests for the recipe! Using macaroni makes this version a nice switch from other chop suey recipes.

PREP: 15 min. **BAKE:** 1 hour

2	pounds pork stew meat
1	package (7 ounces) shell macaroni, cooked and drained
2	cups diced celery
2	medium onions, diced
1	cup chopped green pepper
1	can (10-3/4 ounces) condensed cream of mushroom soup, undiluted
1	can (10-3/4 ounces) condensed cream of chicken soup, undiluted
1	can (4 ounces) mushroom stems and pieces, drained
1/4	cup soy sauce
1	jar (2 ounces) diced pimientos, drained
2	cups chow mein noodles

In a large skillet cook the pork over medium heat until meat is no longer pink; drain. Stir in the next nine ingredients.

Pour into a greased 13-in. x 9-in. x 2-in. baking dish. Top with chow mein noodles. Bake, uncovered, at 350° for 1 to 1-1/4 hours or until pork is tender. YIELD: 8 SERVINGS.

Slow-Cooked Ham 'n' Broccoli

JILL PENNINGTON • JACKSONVILLE, FLORIDA

This sensational dish is so wonderful to come home to, especially on a cool fall or winter day. It's a delicious way to use up leftover holiday ham.

PREP: 10 min. **COOK:** 2 hours + standing

3	cups cubed fully cooked ham
3	cups frozen chopped broccoli, thawed
1	can (10-3/4 ounces) condensed cream of mushroom soup, undiluted
1	jar (8 ounces) process cheese sauce
1	can (8 ounces) sliced water chestnuts, drained
1-1/4	cups uncooked instant rice
1	cup milk
1	celery rib, chopped
1	medium onion, chopped
1/8	to 1/4 teaspoon pepper
1/2	teaspoon paprika

In a 3-qt. slow cooker, combine the first 10 ingredients; mix well. Cover and cook on high for 2-3 hours or until the rice is tender. Let stand for 10 minutes before serving. Sprinkle with paprika. YIELD: 6-8 SERVINGS.

Sausage Mushroom Manicotti

KATHY TAIPALE • IRON RIVER, WISCONSIN

If you're tired of pasta with tomato sauce, try this tasty twist instead. A creamy white sauce covering sausage-filled noodles makes it hard to resist.

PREP: 20 min. **BAKE:** 30 min.

1	package (8 ounces) manicotti shells
1	pound bulk Italian sausage
1/2	cup thinly sliced green onions
1	garlic clove, minced
2	tablespoons butter
1	jar (4-1/2 ounces) sliced mushrooms, drained
1	can (10-3/4 ounces) condensed cream of mushroom soup, undiluted
1/2	cup sour cream
1/4	teaspoon pepper

SAUCE:

- 1 can (5 ounces) evaporated milk
- 1 jar (4-1/2 ounces) sliced mushrooms, drained
- 1 tablespoon minced fresh parsley
- 2 cups (8 ounces) shredded part-skim mozzarella cheese, *divided*

Cook manicotti shells according to package directions. Meanwhile, in a skillet, cook sausage over medium heat until no longer pink; drain and set aside. In the same skillet, saute onions and garlic in butter until tender. Add mushrooms; heat through. Drain shells and set aside.

Transfer mushroom mixture to a bowl; stir in the sausage, soup, sour cream and pepper. Stuff into manicotti shells. Place in a greased 13-in. x 9-in. x 2-in. baking dish.

For sauce, in a saucepan, heat the milk, mushrooms and parsley. Remove from the heat; add 1-1/2 cups cheese, stirring until melted. Pour over stuffed shells.

Cover and bake at 350° for 25 minutes. Uncover; sprinkle with remaining cheese. Bake 5-10 minutes longer or until cheese is melted. YIELD: 7 SERVINGS.

Pork Potpie

DLORES DEWITT • COLORADO SPRINGS, COLORADO

What a great way to use up leftover pork roast—and it sure doesn't taste like leftovers. It's one of those down-home comfort foods that really warms up a cold night.

PREP: 20 min. **BAKE:** 25 min.

- 2 medium carrots, thinly sliced
- 1 small onion, chopped
- 1/4 cup water
- 2 cups cubed cooked pork
- 1 can (10-3/4 ounces) condensed cream of celery soup, undiluted
- 2 tablespoons minced fresh parsley
- 1/4 teaspoon salt
- 1/8 teaspoon dried savory
- 1/8 teaspoon garlic powder
- Pastry for single-crust pie (9 inches)
- 1 tablespoon grated Parmesan cheese

In a saucepan, cook carrots and onion in water until tender; drain. Add the pork, soup, parsley, salt, savory and garlic powder. Transfer to a greased 9-in. pie plate.

On a lightly floured surface, roll out pastry into 10-in. circle; place over pork mixture. Cut slits in top; flute edges. Sprinkle with Parmesan cheese. Bake at 425° for 18-20 minutes or until golden brown. Let pie stand for 5 minutes before cutting. YIELD: 4-6 SERVINGS.

Baked Rice With Sausage

NAOMI FLOOD • EMPORIA, KANSAS

This recipe is great for church suppers or other get-togethers because it produces a big batch and has flavors with broad appeal. Most folks can't guess that the secret ingredient is chicken noodle soup mix.

PREP: 30 min. **BAKE:** 50 min. + standing

- 2 pounds bulk Italian sausage
- 4 celery ribs, thinly sliced
- 1 large onion, chopped
- 1 large green pepper, chopped
- 4-1/2 cups water
- 3/4 cup dry chicken noodle soup mix
- 1 can (10-3/4 ounces) condensed cream of chicken soup, undiluted
- 1 cup uncooked long grain rice
- 1/4 cup dry bread crumbs
- 2 tablespoons butter, melted

In a large skillet, cook the sausage, celery, onion and green pepper over medium heat until meat is no longer pink and vegetables are tender; drain. In a large saucepan, bring water to a boil; add dry soup mix. Reduce heat; simmer, uncovered, for 5 minutes or until the noodles are tender. Stir in cream of chicken soup, rice and sausage mixture; mix well.

Transfer to a greased 13-in. x 9-in. x 2-in. baking dish. Cover and bake at 350° for 40 minutes. Toss bread crumbs and butter; sprinkle over rice mixture. Bake, uncovered, for 10-15 minutes or until rice is tender. Let casserole stand for 10 minutes before serving. YIELD: 12-14 SERVINGS.

baked rice with sausage

Herb Dumplings With Pork Chops

CHERYL ONKEN • WILTON, IOWA

My husband and I grew up on farms. This country-style recipe, starring moist pork chops and tender, homemade dumplings, reminds me of home.

PREP: 20 min. **COOK:** 30 min.

- 1   can (10-3/4 ounces) condensed cream of mushroom soup, undiluted
- 1   can (4 ounces) mushroom stems and pieces, undrained
- 1/2   cup water
- 1/2   teaspoon rubbed sage
- 6   bone-in pork loin chops (1/2 inch thick and 8 ounces *each*)
- 2   tablespoons vegetable oil
- 1   medium onion, sliced

DUMPLINGS:
- 1-1/2   cups all-purpose flour
- 2   teaspoons baking powder
- 3/4   teaspoon salt
- 1/2   teaspoon celery seed
- 1/2   teaspoon rubbed sage
- 3   tablespoons shortening
- 3/4   cup milk
- 1   tablespoon minced fresh parsley

In a large bowl, combine the cream of mushroom soup, mushrooms, water and sage; set aside. In a large skillet, brown the pork chops on both sides in oil; top with onion. Pour soup mixture over top. Bring to a boil; reduce heat.

For dumplings, in a small bowl, combine the flour, baking powder, salt, celery seed and sage. Cut in shortening until mixture resembles coarse crumbs. Stir in milk just until moistened.

Drop dough by 1/4 cupfuls onto simmering soup mixture; sprinkle with parsley. Simmer, uncovered, for 15 minutes. Cover and simmer 15 minutes longer or until a toothpick inserted in a dumpling comes out clean (do not lift cover while simmering). YIELD: 6 SERVINGS.

herb dumplings with pork chops

Pizza Rigatoni

MARILYN COWAN • NORTH MANCHESTER, INDIANA

Turn your slow cooker into a pizzeria with this zesty layered casserole. It is loaded with mozzarella cheese, Italian sausage, pepperoni and pasta.

PREP: 15 min. **COOK:** 4 hours

- 1-1/2   pounds bulk Italian sausage
- 3   cups uncooked rigatoni *or* large tube pasta
- 4   cups (16 ounces) shredded part-skim mozzarella cheese
- 1   can (10-3/4 ounces) condensed cream of mushroom soup, undiluted
- 1   small onion, chopped
- 2   cans (one 15 ounces, one 8 ounces) pizza sauce
- 1   package (3-1/2 ounces) sliced pepperoni
- 1   can (6 ounces) pitted ripe olives, drained and halved

In a skillet, cook sausage until no longer pink; drain. Cook pasta according to package directions; drain.

In a 5-qt. slow cooker, layer half of the sausage, pasta, cheese, soup, onion, pizza sauce, pepperoni and olives. Repeat layers. Cover and cook on low for 4 hours. YIELD: 6-8 SERVINGS.

Country Skillet

TERRI ADRIAN • LAKE CITY, FLORIDA

When I need a fast, flavorful meal-in-one, I turn to this filling combination of kielbasa, rice and veggies. It is an ideal dish for cooler autumn days.

PREP/TOTAL TIME: 30 min.

1   pound fully cooked kielbasa *or* Polish
     sausage, cut into 1/2-inch slices
1/2 cup chopped onion
1   tablespoon vegetable oil
1-1/2 cups water
1   can (10-3/4 ounces) condensed cream
     of celery soup, undiluted
1/2 teaspoon dried basil
1/4 teaspoon dried thyme
1/4 teaspoon pepper
1   package (10 ounces) frozen cut
     broccoli, thawed
1   jar (4-1/2 ounces) sliced mushrooms,
     drained
1   cup uncooked instant rice
1/4 cup grated Parmesan cheese

In a large skillet, cook sausage and onion in oil until onion is tender; drain. Combine the water, soup, basil, thyme and pepper; add to skillet.

Stir in broccoli and mushrooms. Bring to a boil. Stir in rice. Cover and remove from the heat. Let stand for 5-7 minutes or until rice is tender. Sprinkle with Parmesan cheese. YIELD: 4-6 SERVINGS.

Dilled Ham on Rice

DEBBY COLE • WOLF CREEK, OREGON

When expecting company, I fix this main dish featuring ham in a rich, creamy sauce. Seasoned with mustard and dill, this entree makes a nice presentation with a tossed green salad, corn and dinner rolls.

PREP/TOTAL TIME: 30 min.

4   cups julienned fully cooked ham
2   tablespoons butter
2   celery ribs, thinly sliced
1   medium onion, chopped
1   cup sliced fresh mushrooms
1   can (10-3/4 ounces) condensed cream
     of chicken soup, undiluted
1/4 to 1/2 cup milk
2   teaspoons prepared mustard
1/4 to 1/2 teaspoon dill weed
1/2 cup sour cream
     Hot cooked rice

In a large skillet, cook ham in butter until lightly browned. Add celery, onion and mushrooms; saute until tender.

Combine the cream of chicken soup, milk, mustard and dill; add to the ham mixture. Bring to a boil; reduce heat. Stir in sour cream; heat through. Serve over rice. YIELD: 6 SERVINGS.

penny casserole

Penny Casserole

JANET WARE NOVOTNY • GRAND ISLAND, NEBRASKA

This budget-friendly hot dish is very homey. If you know time will be short, boil up the potatoes the day before. That way you can just assemble and bake it the day you serve it.

PREP: 25 min. **BAKE:** 25 min.

1-1/4 pounds red potatoes, cubed
10   hot dogs (1 pound), sliced
2   tablespoons diced onion
1   cup frozen peas, thawed
1   can (10-3/4 ounces) condensed cream
     of mushroom soup, undiluted
3   tablespoons butter, melted
1   tablespoon prepared mustard
1/8 teaspoon pepper

In a saucepan, cook the potatoes in boiling salted water until tender; drain. In a greased 2-1/2-qt. baking dish, combine the potatoes, hot dogs, onion and peas. Combine cream of mushroom soup, butter, mustard and pepper; gently stir into the potato mixture. Bake, uncovered, at 350° for 25 minutes or until heated through. YIELD: 6-8 SERVINGS.

cooking tip

Penny Casserole is a quick supper that is perfect for a busy weeknight. Plus, you can easily modify the versatile recipe to suit your family's tastes. Simply substitute a package of frozen corn, green beans or broccoli for the peas.

sausage rice casserole

Sausage Rice Casserole

JENNIFER TROST • WEST LINN, OREGON

I fiddled around with this dish, trying to adjust it to my family's tastes. When my pickiest child cleaned her plate, I knew I'd found the right flavor combination.

PREP: 30 min. **BAKE:** 40 min.

2	packages (7.2 ounces *each*) rice pilaf
2	pounds bulk pork sausage
6	celery ribs, chopped
4	medium carrots, sliced
1	can (10-3/4 ounces) condensed cream of chicken soup, undiluted
1	can (10-3/4 ounces) condensed cream of mushroom soup, undiluted
2	teaspoons onion powder
1/2	teaspoon garlic powder
1/4	teaspoon pepper

Prepare rice mixes according to package directions. Meanwhile, in a large skillet, cook the sausage, celery and carrots over medium heat until meat is no longer pink; drain.

In a large bowl, combine the sausage mixture, rice, soups, onion powder, garlic powder and pepper. Transfer to two greased 11-in. x 7-in. x 2-in. baking dishes.

Cover and freeze one casserole for up to 3 months. Cover and bake remaining casserole at 350° for 40-45 minutes or until vegetables are tender.

To use frozen casserole: Thaw casserole in the refrigerator overnight. Remove from the refrigerator 30 minutes before baking. Bake as directed. YIELD: 2 CASSEROLES (6-8 SERVINGS EACH).

Apple Pork Chop Casserole

BEVERLY BAXTER • KANSAS CITY, KANSAS

I've loved this recipe since the first time I tried it. The apples and raisins give a nice flavor to the stuffing.

PREP: 30 min. **BAKE:** 30 min.

2	boneless pork loin chops (3/4 inch thick)
2	teaspoons vegetable oil
3/4	cup water
1	tablespoon butter
1	small tart green apple, chopped
2	tablespoons raisins
1-1/2	cups crushed chicken stuffing mix
2/3	cup condensed cream of mushroom soup, undiluted

In a skillet, brown meat in oil for about 5 minutes on each side.

In a saucepan, combine the water, butter, apple and raisins; bring to a boil. Stir in stuffing mix. Remove from the heat; cover and let stand for 5 minutes. Fluff with a fork.

Transfer to a greased shallow 1-qt. baking dish. Top with meat. Spoon soup over meat and stuffing. Cover and bake at 350° for 30-35 minutes or until a meat thermometer inserted into pork chops reads 160° to 170°. YIELD: 2 SERVINGS.

Cheesy Bratwurst

KIM MIERS • ROCK ISLAND, ILLINOIS

I'll admit that the combination of ingredients in this recipe is unusual, but I guarantee the flavor is fabulous!

PREP: 10 min. **COOK:** 35 min.

4	medium potatoes, peeled and cut into 1/2-inch cubes
2	cups water, *divided*
6	fully cooked bratwurst links (1 pound), cut into 1/2-inch slices
1	can (10-3/4 ounces) condensed cream of mushroom soup, undiluted
2	cups frozen cut green beans
1	small onion, chopped
1	cup (4 ounces) shredded cheddar cheese

Place potatoes and 1 cup water in a deep skillet or large saucepan; cook for 15 minutes or until potatoes are almost tender. Drain and set aside.

In the same pan, brown bratwurst. Add soup, beans, onion, potatoes and remaining water. Cover and simmer for 15 minutes or until the vegetables are tender. Stir in the cheese; heat until cheese is melted. YIELD: 6 SERVINGS.

Stuffed Pork Chops

LINDA MARTIN • BARTLETT, TENNESSEE

My husband and I enjoyed these hearty pork chops at a restaurant in Bull Shoals, Arkansas. The combination of flavors and creamy sauce is unbeatable.

PREP: 15 min. **BAKE:** 40 min.

4	pork chops (1 inch thick)
2	tablespoons vegetable oil
3	cups day-old French bread cubes (1/2 inch)
1/4	cup butter, melted
1/4	cup chicken broth
2	tablespoons chopped celery
2	tablespoons chopped onion
1/4	teaspoon poultry seasoning
1	can (10-3/4 ounces) condensed cream of mushroom soup, undiluted
1/3	cup water

In a skillet, brown the pork chops in oil. Place chops in an ungreased shallow baking pan. Toss bread cubes, butter, broth, celery, onion and poultry seasoning. Mound about 1/2 cup stuffing on each pork chop.

Combine soup and water; pour over chops. Cover and bake at 350° for 30 minutes. Uncover; bake for 10-15 minutes longer or until juices run clear and a meat thermometer reads 160° to 170°. YIELD: 4 SERVINGS.

cooking tip

The thickness of pork chops affects the cooking time. For thinner chops, reduce the cooking time. For thicker chops, check doneness at the minimum time and if necessary, cook them a little longer.

Zucchini Pork Chop Supper

LINDA MARTIN • RHINEBECK, NEW YORK

My mom gave me the recipe for a zucchini casserole. I added the meat because I was trying to make a one-dish supper. Now, I look forward to fresh zucchini.

PREP: 10 min. **BAKE:** 1 hour

1	package (14 ounces) seasoned cubed stuffing mix, *divided*
1/4	cup butter, melted
2	pounds zucchini, cut into 1/2-inch pieces
1/2	cup grated carrots
1	can (10-3/4 ounces) condensed cream of celery soup, undiluted
1/2	cup milk
1	cup (8 ounces) sour cream
1	tablespoon chopped fresh parsley *or* 1 teaspoon dried parsley flakes
1/2	teaspoon pepper
	Water *or* additional milk
6	pork loin chops (1 inch thick and 8 ounces *each*)

In a large bowl, combine two-thirds of the stuffing mix with butter; place half in a greased 13-in. x 9-in. x 2-in. baking dish. In another large bowl, combine the zucchini, carrots, soup, milk, sour cream, parsley and pepper; spoon over stuffing. Sprinkle remaining buttered stuffing on top.

Crush remaining stuffing mix; place in a shallow bowl. In another shallow bowl, add the water or milk. Dip pork chops in water or milk then roll in stuffing crumbs.

Place pork on top of stuffing mixture. Bake, uncovered, at 350° for 1 hour or until a meat thermometer reads 160° to 170°. YIELD: 6 SERVINGS.

zucchini pork chop supper

Pork Chop Potato Bake

ARDIS HENNING • MONTELLO, WISCONSIN

Folks who sample my cooking tease me and say I should open a restaurant. But I am more than happy just cooking delicious meals like this time-honored dish for my family and friends.

PREP: 15 min. **BAKE:** 1-1/4 hours

6	pork chops (5 ounces *each*), trimmed
1	can (10-3/4 ounces) condensed cream of mushroom soup, undiluted
1	can (4 ounces) sliced mushrooms, drained
1/4	cup chicken broth
1/2	teaspoon garlic salt
1/2	teaspoon Worcestershire sauce
1/4	teaspoon dried thyme
1	can (16 ounces) whole potatoes, drained
1	package (10 ounces) frozen peas, thawed
1	tablespoon diced pimientos

In a large skillet coated with cooking spray, brown pork chops on each side. Place chops in an ungreased 13-in. x 9-in. x 2-in. baking pan. Combine the next six ingredients; mix well. Pour over pork. Cover and bake at 350° for 1 hour. Add potatoes, peas and pimientos. Cover and bake 15 minutes longer or until pork is tender and vegetables are heated through. YIELD: 6 SERVINGS.

pork chop potato bake

ham pasties

Ham Pasties

DELORES YUNG • WATROUS, SASKATCHEWAN

You'll find these in my recipe file under "F"—for "favorites!" My family is always delighted to see these savory, ham-filled delicacies on the table.

PREP: 40 min. + chilling **BAKE:** 15 min.

5	cups all-purpose flour
1	tablespoon brown sugar
1	teaspoon salt
1/2	teaspoon baking powder
1	pound shortening
1/2	to 3/4 cup cold water
1	egg, beaten
2	teaspoons white vinegar

FILLING:

3	cups diced fully cooked ham (1/4-inch pieces)
2	tablespoons diced green pepper
2	tablespoons diced pimientos
1	tablespoon minced onion
1	can (10-3/4 ounces) condensed cream of mushroom soup, undiluted

GLAZE:

1	egg
1	tablespoon water

Poppy seeds *or* sesame seeds

In a large bowl, combine flour, brown sugar, salt and baking powder. Cut in shortening, half at a time, until crumbly. Combine 1/2 cup water, egg and vinegar; add all at once to flour mixture and toss with a fork until dough forms a ball. Add remaining water only if necessary. Wrap tightly and refrigerate for several hours.

Meanwhile, combine all filling ingredients. On a lightly floured surface, roll out one-fourth of the dough to 1/8-in. thickness. Using a 3-1/2- to 4-in. round cutter, cut dough into circles. Place on ungreased baking sheets.

Spread about 1 tablespoon of filling on half of each circle. Moisten edge slightly with water and fold over, sealing edges with a fork. Cut slits in top of pasties.

Repeat with remaining dough and filling. In a small bowl, beat egg with water; brush tops of pasties. Sprinkle with poppy or sesame seeds. Bake at 400° for 15-20 minutes or until golden. Serve warm. YIELD: 3-1/2 TO 4-1/2 DOZEN.

One-Pot Ham Dinner

JODY COHEN • MACKEYVILLE, PENNSYLVANIA

Looking for a speedy skillet supper? Simply add potatoes and green beans to ham steak before topping off this down-home creation with a comforting mushroom sauce. Dinner is served in no time.

PREP: 15 min. **COOK:** 45 min.

1	fully cooked ham slice (1 to 1-1/2 pounds)
4	medium potatoes, peeled and sliced
1/4	to 1/2 teaspoon salt
1/4	teaspoon pepper
2	cups frozen cut green beans
1	medium onion, thinly sliced
1	can (10-3/4 ounces) condensed cream of mushroom soup, undiluted
1/2	cup water

In a large skillet over medium heat, brown the ham slice. Arrange potatoes over ham; sprinkle with salt and pepper. Top with beans and onion. Combine soup and water; pour over all. Cook for 2 minutes. Reduce heat; cover and simmer for 45-50 minutes or until potatoes are tender. YIELD: 4 SERVINGS.

cooking tip

As if One-Pot Ham Dinner wasn't easy enough already, it can be on the table even faster when you don't have to peel and slice the potatoes. Instead, use a bag of frozen cubed potatoes found in the freezer section at your grocery store.

wild rice & ham casserole

Wild Rice & Ham Casserole

STACEY DIEHL • LECANTO, FLORIDA

My grandmother gave me this recipe. The blend of flavors is fantastic. It's so simple to make and can easily be doubled for a large gathering.

PREP: 15 min. **BAKE:** 45 min.

1	package (6-1/4 ounces) quick-cooking long grain and wild rice mix
1	package (10 ounces) frozen cut broccoli, thawed and drained
2	cups cubed fully cooked ham
1	can (10-3/4 ounces) condensed cream of mushroom soup, undiluted
1	cup mayonnaise
2	teaspoons prepared mustard
1	cup (4 ounces) shredded cheddar cheese

Prepare the rice according to package directions. Spoon into an ungreased 2-1/2-qt. baking dish. Top rice with broccoli and ham. Combine the cream of mushroom soup, mayonnaise and mustard. Spread over rice mixture and mix gently.

Cover and bake at 350° for 45 minutes or until bubbly. Sprinkle with cheese. Let casserole stand for 5 minutes before serving. YIELD: 6 SERVINGS.

au gratin ham potpie

Au Gratin Ham Potpie

MARY ZINSMEISTER • SLINGER, WISCONSIN

I first had this dish when my aunt made it for a family get-together. The entire gang loved it and everyone was so happy when she shared the recipe. Now, I make it almost every time there is extra ham on hand.

PREP: 15 min. **BAKE:** 40 min.

1	package (4.9 ounces) au gratin potatoes
1-1/2	cups boiling water
2	cups frozen peas and carrots
1-1/2	cups cubed fully cooked ham
1	can (10-3/4 ounces) condensed cream of chicken soup, undiluted
1	can (4 ounces) mushroom stems and pieces, drained
1/2	cup milk
1/2	cup sour cream
1	jar (2 ounces) diced pimientos, drained
1	sheet refrigerated pie pastry

In a large bowl, combine the potatoes, contents of sauce mix, boiling water, peas and carrots, ham, soup, mushrooms, milk, sour cream and pimientos. Pour into an ungreased 2-qt. round baking dish.

Roll out pastry to fit top of dish; place over potato mixture. Flute edges; cut slits in pastry. Bake at 400° for 40-45 minutes or until golden brown. Let stand for 5 minutes before serving. YIELD: 4-6 SERVINGS.

Saucy Sausage & Veggies

JANICE ROSE • ABILENE, KANSAS

This saucy casserole calls for a broccoli-carrot-water chestnut blend, but feel free to use whatever frozen mixed vegetables you prefer instead.

PREP: 15 min. **BAKE:** 45 min.

2	packages (1 pound *each*) frozen mixed broccoli, carrots and water chestnuts, thawed
1	pound fully cooked smoked sausage, cut into 1/2-inch pieces
1	can (10-3/4 ounces) condensed cream of celery soup, undiluted
1/2	cup whole kernel corn, drained
3/4	cup milk
3/4	cup cubed process American cheese (Velveeta)
1/2	teaspoon pepper
1/2	cup sour cream
1/2	cup seasoned dry bread crumbs
2	tablespoons butter, melted

Place vegetables in a greased 11-in. x 7-in. x 2-in. baking dish. In a skillet, brown sausage; drain. Layer over the vegetables.

In a saucepan, combine soup, milk, cheese and pepper. Cook over low heat until cheese is melted; remove from the heat. Stir in sour cream; pour over the vegetables and sausage.

Combine bread crumbs and butter; sprinkle over casserole. Bake, uncovered, at 350° for 45 minutes or until browned and bubbly. YIELD: 6-8 SERVINGS.

cooking tip

Don't care for sausage? Saucy Sausage & Veggies is just as tasty using cubed cooked chicken or ham. Make dinner even easier by buying prepackaged containers of cooked cubed chicken or ham at the grocery store.

potato ham bake

Potato Ham Bake

ARTHUR HEIDORN • HILLSIDE, ILLINOIS

I like to make this hearty delight with the leftovers from a baked ham. It's a great meal all by itself.

PREP: 10 min. **BAKE:** 1 hour 25 min.

3	medium potatoes, peeled and thinly sliced
2	cups cubed fully cooked ham
1	medium onion, sliced and separated into rings
8	slices process American cheese
1	can (10-3/4 ounces) condensed cream of mushroom soup, undiluted
1/2	cup frozen peas, thawed

In a greased 3-qt. baking dish, layer half of the potatoes, ham, onion, cheese and soup. Repeat layers. Cover and bake at 350° for 1-1/4 hours or until the potatoes are almost tender.

Sprinkle with peas. Bake, uncovered, for 10 minutes or until heated through. YIELD: 6 SERVINGS.

Pork & Green Chili Casserole

DIANNE ESPOSITE • NEW MIDDLETOWN, OHIO

I'm always on the lookout for good, quick recipes to fix for my hungry bunch. This zippy one-dish wonder was brought to a picnic at my house. People raved over it.

PREP: 20 min. **BAKE:** 30 min.

1-1/2	pounds boneless pork, cut into 1/2-inch cubes
1	tablespoon vegetable oil
1	can (15 ounces) black beans, rinsed and drained
1	can (10-3/4 ounces) condensed cream of chicken soup, undiluted
1	can (14-1/2 ounces) diced tomatoes, undrained
2	cans (4 ounces *each*) chopped green chilies
1	cup quick-cooking brown rice
1/4	cup water
2	to 3 tablespoons salsa
1	teaspoon ground cumin
1/2	cup shredded cheddar cheese

In a large skillet, saute pork in oil until no longer pink; drain. Add the black beans, cream of chicken soup, tomatoes, chilies, rice, water, salsa and cumin; cook and stir until bubbly.

Pour into an ungreased 2-qt. baking dish. Bake, uncovered, at 350° for 30 minutes or until bubbly. Sprinkle with cheese; let stand a few minutes before serving. YIELD: 6 SERVINGS.

pork & green chili casserole

Ham 'n' Tater Bake

PEGGY GRIEME • PINEHURST, NORTH CAROLINA

This ham and potato medley reminds me of a loaded baked potato. I usually make it several times a month, and I've even served it to company. I'm always asked for the recipe, which I received from my sister.

PREP: 10 min. **BAKE:** 40 min.

    1   package (28 ounces) frozen steak fries
    3   cups frozen chopped broccoli, thawed
            and drained
 1-1/2   cups diced fully cooked ham
    1   can (10-3/4 ounces) condensed cream
            of broccoli soup, undiluted
   3/4   cup milk
   1/2   cup mayonnaise
    1   cup (4 ounces) shredded cheddar
            cheese

Arrange fries in a greased 3-qt. baking dish; layer with broccoli and then ham. Combine the soup, milk and mayonnaise until smooth; pour over ham.

Cover and bake at 350° for 20 minutes. Sprinkle with cheese; bake, uncovered, 20-25 minutes longer or until bubbly. YIELD: 6-8 SERVINGS.

EDITOR'S NOTE: Reduced-fat or fat-free mayonnaise is not recommended for this recipe.

ham & chicken casserole

Ham & Chicken Casserole

CONNIE SANDEN • MENTOR, OHIO

This recipe has traveled to many parts of the country. That's because I've served it to guests from Washington to New Hampshire. My grown children all have a copy of the recipe, so they can enjoy this winning dish with their families, too.

PREP: 25 min. **BAKE:** 45 min.

    1   cup chopped onion
    2   tablespoons butter
    2   cups cubed fully cooked ham
    2   cups diced cooked chicken
    1   medium green pepper, chopped
   1/2   cup chopped sweet red pepper
    1   cup whole pimento-stuffed green
            olives
    1   can (10-3/4 ounces) condensed cream
            of mushroom soup, undiluted
    1   cup (8 ounces) sour cream
 1-1/2   teaspoons salt
   1/4   teaspoon pepper
    8   ounces noodles, cooked and drained
    3   tablespoons shredded Parmesan
            cheese

In a skillet, saute onion in butter until tender. In a large bowl, combine the ham, chicken, peppers, olives, soup, sour cream, salt, pepper and onion. Fold in noodles.

Pour into a greased 2-1/2-qt. baking dish. Sprinkle with the Parmesan cheese. Bake, uncovered, at 325° for 45 minutes or until bubbly. YIELD: 8 SERVINGS.

ham 'n' tater bake

Ham Tetrazzini

SUSAN BLAIR • STERLING, MICHIGAN

I modified a recipe that came with my slow cooker to reduce the fat without sacrificing any of the flavor. I've served this at parties, family gatherings and potlucks. Everyone is pleasantly surprised to find that what they are eating is actually healthy.

PREP: 15 min. **COOK:** 4 hours

1	can (10-3/4 ounces) reduced-sodium condensed cream of mushroom soup, undiluted
1	cup sliced fresh mushrooms
1	cup cubed fully cooked lean ham
1/2	cup fat-free evaporated milk
2	tablespoons white wine *or* water
1	teaspoon prepared horseradish
1	package (7 ounces) spaghetti
1/2	cup shredded Parmesan cheese

In a 3-qt. slow cooker, combine the soup, mushrooms, ham, milk, wine or water and horseradish. Cover and cook on low for 4 hours. Cook spaghetti according to package directions; drain. Add the spaghetti and cheese to slow cooker; toss to coat. YIELD: 6 SERVINGS.

sausage & mushroom stew

Sausage & Mushroom Stew

ANN NACE • PERKASIE, PENNSYLVANIA

The perfect meal for a hungry, hardworking bunch, this savory combo has generous chunks of sausage and veggies and a delicious, rich sauce. Lots of color adds plenty of interest to each ladleful.

PREP: 10 min. **BAKE:** 1-3/4 min.

2	cans (10-3/4 ounces *each*) condensed cream of mushroom soup, undiluted
1-1/2	pounds smoked kielbasa, cut into 1-inch rounds
5	medium potatoes, peeled and cut into 1-inch chunks
4	carrots, peeled and cut into 1-inch pieces
3	medium onions, coarsely chopped
1	cup fresh green beans, halved
3/4	pound fresh mushrooms, halved
1/2	medium head cabbage, coarsely chopped

In an ovenproof 5-qt. Dutch oven or baking dish, combine the first seven ingredients. Cover and bake at 350° for 1-1/4 hours.

Uncover and stir. Add the cabbage. Cover and bake 30 minutes longer or until vegetables are tender. Stir again before serving. YIELD: 6-8 SERVINGS.

Stovetop Bratwurst Dinner

DARCY DOUGHERTY • POTSVILLE, IOWA

For a lip-smacking change from plain brats, try combining them with green beans and a mild cheese sauce for a swift skillet supper. I round out the menu with a vegetable salad and brownies for dessert.

PREP/TOTAL TIME: 30 min.

1-1/2	cups milk
1	can (10-3/4 ounces) condensed cream of mushroom soup, undiluted
1	pound fully cooked bratwurst links, cut into 1/2-inch pieces
2	cups frozen cut green beans
4	ounces process cheese (Velveeta), cubed
6	cups hot cooked noodles

In a large saucepan, combine the milk and soup until blended. Add bratwurst and beans. Bring to a boil. Reduce heat; cover and simmer for 15 minutes or until heated through. Stir in cheese until melted. Serve over noodles. YIELD: 4-6 SERVINGS.

CHAPTER 6
Chicken & Turkey

Pineapple Chicken Casserole

SUSAN WARREN • NORTH MANCHESTER, INDIANA

I love to cook, but with juggling my husband's and teenage twins' schedules, I have little time to spend in the kitchen. That's why this dish is a lifesaver!

PREP/TOTAL TIME: 30 min.

- 2   cups cubed cooked chicken
- 1   can (10-3/4 ounces) condensed cream of mushroom soup, undiluted
- 1   cup pineapple tidbits
- 2   celery ribs, chopped
- 1   tablespoon chopped green onion
- 1   tablespoon soy sauce
- 1   can (3 ounces) chow mein noodles, *divided*

In a large bowl, combine the first six ingredients. Fold in 1 cup chow mein noodles. Transfer to a greased shallow 2-qt. baking dish. Sprinkle with remaining noodles. Bake, uncovered, at 350° for 20-25 minutes or until heated through. YIELD: 4-6 SERVINGS.

Stuffed Pasta Shells

JUDY MEMO • NEW CASTLE, PENNSYLVANIA

This is a different way to use up leftovers. A casserole of pasta shells filled with moist stuffing, tender chicken chunks and green peas is covered with an easy sauce.

PREP: 15 min. **BAKE:** 30 min.

- 1-1/2 cups cooked stuffing
- 2   cups diced cooked chicken *or* turkey
- 1/2   cup frozen peas, thawed
- 1/2   cup mayonnaise
- 18   jumbo pasta shells, cooked and drained
- 1   can (10-3/4 ounces) condensed cream of chicken soup, undiluted
- 2/3   cup water
  Paprika
  Minced fresh parsley

In a large bowl, combine the stuffing, chicken, peas and mayonnaise; spoon into pasta shells. Place in a greased 13-in. x 9-in. x 2-in. baking dish. In a small bowl, combine soup and water; pour over shells. Sprinkle with paprika.

Cover and bake at 350° for 30 minutes or until heated through. Sprinkle with minced fresh parsley. YIELD: 6 SERVINGS.

rotini chicken casserole

Rotini Chicken Casserole

RUTH LEE • TROY, ONTARIO

Pasta bakes are a reliable standby in our family. I changed the original recipe for this entree to suit our tastes...we all think it's absolutely delicious.

PREP: 15 min. **BAKE:** 25 min.

- 2-3/4 cups uncooked tricolor rotini *or* spiral pasta
- 3/4   cup chopped onion
- 1/2   cup chopped celery
- 2   garlic cloves, minced
- 1   tablespoon olive oil
- 3   cups cubed cooked chicken breast
- 1   can (10-3/4 ounces) reduced-fat reduced-sodium condensed cream of chicken soup, undiluted
- 1-1/2 cups fat-free milk
- 1   package (16 ounces) frozen Italian-blend vegetables
- 1   cup (4 ounces) shredded reduced-fat cheddar cheese
- 2   tablespoons minced fresh parsley
- 1-1/4 teaspoons dried thyme
- 1   teaspoon salt
- 2/3   cup crushed cornflakes

Cook pasta according to package directions. Meanwhile, in a nonstick skillet, saute onion, celery and garlic in oil until tender. Drain pasta; place in a bowl. Add the onion mixture, chicken, soup, milk, frozen vegetables, cheese, parsley, thyme and salt.

Pour into a shallow 3-qt. baking dish coated with cooking spray. Cover and bake at 350° for 25 minutes. Sprinkle with cornflakes; spritz with cooking spray. Bake, uncovered, 10-15 minutes longer or until heated through. YIELD: 8 SERVINGS.

artichoke chicken

chicken. Combine the soup, mayonnaise, lemon juice and curry; pour over the chicken. Sprinkle with cheddar cheese. Combine the bread crumbs, Parmesan cheese and butter; sprinkle over top.

Bake, uncovered, at 350° for 30-35 minutes or until bubbly. YIELD: 6-8 SERVINGS.

EDITOR'S NOTE: Reduced-fat or fat-free mayonnaise is not recommended for this recipe.

Saucy Macaroni Skillet

LINDA STEVENS • MADISON, ALABAMA

This creamy skillet sensation takes mac-and-cheese recipes to a brand-new level. Chock-full of turkey, fresh vegetables and crunchy almonds, it's one satisfying entree I can pop in the oven or prepare just as successfully on the stovetop.

PREP/TOTAL TIME: 25 min.

1-1/2	cups uncooked elbow macaroni
4	celery ribs, chopped
1/2	cup chopped green pepper
1/4	cup chopped onion
1/4	cup butter, cubed
2	cans (10-3/4 ounces *each*) condensed cream of chicken soup, undiluted
2/3	cup milk
2	cups (8 ounces) shredded cheddar cheese
3	cups cubed cooked turkey *or* chicken
1	jar (4 ounces) diced pimientos, drained
1/2	teaspoon salt
1/4	teaspoon ground nutmeg
1/2	cup sliced almonds, toasted

Cook the macaroni according to the package directions. Meanwhile, in a large saucepan, saute the celery, green pepper and onion in butter until tender. Stir in soup and milk until blended. Add the cheese; cook and stir over medium heat until melted.

Drain macaroni. Add the macaroni, turkey, pimientos, salt and nutmeg to the soup mixture; cook and stir until heated through. Sprinkle with almonds. YIELD: 6 SERVINGS.

Artichoke Chicken

ROBERTA GREEN • HEMET, CALIFORNIA

This recipe has evolved through generations to satisfy my family's fondness for artichokes. I enjoy preparing this one-dish favorite for casual suppers as well as special-occasion celebrations.

PREP: 10 min. **BAKE:** 30 min.

2	cans (14 ounces *each*) water-packed artichoke hearts, rinsed, drained and quartered
2	tablespoons olive oil
3	garlic cloves, minced
2-2/3	cups cubed cooked chicken
2	cans (10-3/4 ounces *each*) condensed cream of chicken soup, undiluted
1	cup mayonnaise
1	teaspoon lemon juice
1/2	teaspoon curry powder
1-1/2	cups (6 ounces) shredded cheddar cheese
1	cup seasoned bread crumbs
1/4	cup grated Parmesan cheese
2	tablespoons butter, melted

In a bowl, combine the artichokes, oil and garlic. Place in a greased 2-1/2-qt. baking dish. Top with

Lasagna Deluxe

BETTY RUTHERFORD • ST. GEORGE, UTAH

You don't need to precook the noodles in this variation of an Italian classic, so it is perfect for family dinners during the week or for lazy weekend meals.

PREP: 20 min. **BAKE:** 1 hour + standing

- 1   cup (8 ounces) 4% cottage cheese
- 1   package (3 ounces) cream cheese, softened
- 1   can (10-3/4 ounces) condensed cream of mushroom soup, undiluted
- 1-1/2   cup chopped fresh broccoli
- 1/2   cup chopped celery
- 1/3   cup chopped onion
- 1/4   cup milk
- 1/2   teaspoon poultry seasoning
- 6   uncooked lasagna noodles
- 1-1/2   cups cubed cooked chicken
- 1/2   cup shredded Monterey Jack cheese
- 2/3   cup boiling water

In a small bowl, combine cottage cheese and cream cheese; set aside. In another bowl, combine the next six ingredients; set aside.

Place two lasagna noodles in a greased 11-in. x 7-in. x 2-in. baking dish. Top with half the cottage cheese mixture and a third of the broccoli mixture. Repeat layers of noodles, cheese and broccoli. Top with two noodles, chicken and remaining broccoli mixture. Sprinkle with Monterey Jack cheese. Pour boiling water around edges of dish.

Cover tightly and bake at 350° for 60-65 minutes. Leave covered and let stand for 10 minutes before serving. YIELD: 6 SERVINGS.

Cashew Chicken Casserole

JULIE RIDLON • SOLWAY, MINNESOTA

I especially like this main dish because I can get it ready the day before. It is easy to whip up thanks to the ingredient list of common pantry items, including macaroni, canned soup and saltine crackers.

PREP: 15 min. **BAKE:** 35 min.

- 2   cups uncooked elbow macaroni
- 3   cups cubed cooked chicken
- 1/2   cup cubed process American cheese
- 1   small onion, chopped
- 1/2   cup chopped celery
- 1/2   cup chopped green pepper
- 1   can (8 ounces) sliced water chestnuts, drained
- 1   can (10-3/4 ounces) condensed cream of mushroom soup, undiluted
- 1   can (10-3/4 ounces) condensed cream of chicken soup, undiluted
- 1-1/3   cups milk
- 1   can (14-1/2 ounces) chicken broth
- 1/4   cup butter, melted

- 2/3   cup crushed saltines (about 20 crackers)
- 3/4   cup cashew halves

In a greased 13-in. x 9-in. x 2-in. baking dish, layer the first seven ingredients in the order listed. In a bowl, combine the soups, milk and broth. Pour over water chestnuts. Cover and refrigerate overnight.

Toss butter and cracker crumbs; sprinkle over casserole. Top with cashews. Bake, uncovered, at 350° for 35-40 minutes or until macaroni is tender. YIELD: 6 SERVINGS.

Stuffing-Topped Chicken & Broccoli

DAR JACKSON • GREENVILLE, SOUTH CAROLINA

People tell me hot and hearty foods like this home-style bake remind them of their mom's cooking. I appreciate how quickly this scrumptious comfort food comes together when I'm in a pinch.

PREP: 15 min. **BAKE:** 45 min.

- 1   package (6 ounces) stuffing mix
- 2   cans (10-3/4 ounces *each*) condensed cream of chicken soup, undiluted
- 1   cup water
- 3   tablespoons sour cream
- 3-1/2   cups cubed cooked chicken
- 2   cups instant rice, cooked
- 2   packages (10 ounces *each*) frozen broccoli cuts, thawed

Prepare stuffing mix according to package directions; set aside. In a large bowl, combine the soup, water and sour cream until blended. Stir in the chicken, rice and broccoli.

Transfer to a greased 3-qt. baking dish. Top cheese mixture with the stuffing. Cover and bake at 350° for 30 minutes. Bake, uncovered, 15-20 minutes longer or until bubbly. YIELD: 8-10 SERVINGS.

stuffing-topped chicken & broccoli

Light Chicken Cordon Bleu

SHANNON STRATE • SALT LAKE CITY, UTAH

I love chicken cordon bleu, but since I'm watching my cholesterol, I couldn't afford to indulge in it often. Then I trimmed down a recipe that I received in my high school home economics class years ago. The creamy sauce makes it extra special.

PREP: 20 min. **BAKE:** 25 min.

8	boneless skinless chicken breast halves (4 ounces *each*)
1/2	teaspoon pepper
8	slices (1 ounce *each*) lean deli ham
1-1/2	cups (6 ounces) shredded part-skim mozzarella cheese
2/3	cup fat-free milk
1	cup crushed cornflakes
1	teaspoon paprika
1/2	teaspoon garlic powder
1/4	teaspoon salt

SAUCE:

1	can (10-3/4 ounces) reduced-fat reduced-sodium condensed cream of chicken soup, undiluted
1/2	cup fat-free sour cream
1	teaspoon lemon juice

Flatten chicken to 1/4-in. thickness. Sprinkle with pepper; place a ham slice and 3 tablespoons of cheese down the center of each piece. Roll up and tuck in ends; secure with toothpicks. Pour milk into a shallow bowl. In another bowl, combine the cornflakes, paprika, garlic powder and salt. Dip chicken in milk, then roll in crumbs.

Place in a 13-in. x 9-in. x 2-in. baking dish coated with cooking spray. Bake, uncovered, at 350° for 25-30 minutes or until juices run clear.

light chicken cordon bleu

Meanwhile, in a small saucepan, whisk the soup, sour cream and lemon juice until blended; heat through. Discard toothpicks from chicken; serve with sauce. YIELD: 8 SERVINGS.

Chow Mein Chicken

DEBBIE FRANZEN • SEWICKLEY, PENNSYLVANIA

If you enjoy Chinese food, you are sure to rave about this flavorful, Asian-inspired dish. Chow mein noodles and cashews give it a delightful crunch.

PREP/TOTAL TIME: 30 min.

2	celery ribs, chopped
1	medium onion, chopped
1/4	cup butter
1	can (10-3/4 ounces) condensed cream of mushroom soup, undiluted
1/2	cup chicken broth
1	tablespoon soy sauce
3	cups cubed cooked chicken
1/2	cup sliced fresh mushrooms
1	can (3 ounces) chow mein noodles
1/3	cup salted cashew halves

In a saucepan, saute celery and onion in butter until tender. Stir in soup, broth and soy sauce. Add the chicken and mushrooms; heat through.

Transfer to a greased 2-qt. baking dish. Sprinkle with chow mein noodles and cashews. Bake, uncovered, at 350° for 15-20 minutes or until heated through. YIELD: 4 SERVINGS.

White Turkey Chili

TINA BARRETT • HOUSTON, TEXAS

I came up with this healthy chili by combining several recipes I liked and changing the flavors until it was just right. You won't believe how simple it is!

PREP/TOTAL TIME: 30 min.

2	cups cubed cooked turkey breast
2	cans (15 ounces each) white kidney *or* cannellini beans, rinsed and drained
1	can (10-3/4 ounces) reduced-fat reduced-sodium condensed cream of chicken soup, undiluted
1-1/3	cups fat-free milk
1	can (4 ounces) chopped green chilies, drained
1	tablespoon dried minced onion

apple turkey potpie

1 tablespoon minced fresh cilantro *or* parsley
1 teaspoon garlic powder
1 teaspoon ground cumin
1 teaspoon dried oregano
6 tablespoons fat-free sour cream

In a large saucepan, combine the first 10 ingredients; bring to a boil. Reduce heat; cover and simmer for 25-30 minutes or until heated through. Garnish with sour cream. YIELD: 6 SERVINGS.

Chicken Broccoli Spaghetti

JEANETTE FUEHRING • CONCORDIA, MISSOURI

This cheesy bake makes enough for two casseroles. I serve one for supper the night I make it and freeze the other for a quick meal on a busy night.

PREP: 25 min. **BAKE:** 30 min. + freezing

1-1/2 pounds boneless skinless chicken breasts
1 package (1 pound) spaghetti
2 cups fresh broccoli florets
1 can (10-3/4 ounces) condensed cream of chicken soup, undiluted
1 can (10-3/4 ounces) condensed cream of mushroom soup, undiluted
1-1/4 cups water
1 pound process cheese (Velveeta), cubed
1/4 teaspoon pepper

Place chicken in a large skillet and cover with water; bring to a boil. Reduce heat; cover and simmer for 12-14 minutes or until juices run clear. Meanwhile, cook spaghetti according to package directions; drain. Drain chicken and cut into cubes; set aside.

In a saucepan, cook broccoli in a small amount of water for 5-8 minutes or until crisp-tender. Drain and set aside. In the same pan, combine soups and water. Stir in cheese; cook and stir until cheese is melted. Add the chicken, broccoli and pepper; heat through. Stir in spaghetti; mix well.

Transfer misxture to two greased 8-in. square baking dishes. Cover one casserole and freeze for up to 3 months. Bake the other casserole, uncovered, at 350° for 30-40 minutes or until lightly browned and edges are bubbly.

To bake frozen casserole: Completely thaw in the refrigerator. Cover and bake at 350° for 45-50 minutes or until heated through. YIELD: 2 CASSEROLES (4-6 SERVINGS EACH).

Apple Turkey Potpie

GEORGIA MACDONALD • DOVER, NEW HAMPSHIRE

I like to take leftover holiday turkey and turn it into this delicious entree. Apples and raisins add a slight sweetness to this wonderful variation on chicken potpie.

PREP: 10 min. **BAKE:** 25 min.

1/4 cup chopped onion
1 tablespoon butter
2 cans (10-3/4 ounces *each*) condensed cream of chicken soup, undiluted
3 cups cubed cooked turkey
1 large unpeeled tart apple, cubed
1/3 cup golden raisins
1 teaspoon lemon juice
1/4 teaspoon ground nutmeg
Pastry for a single-crust pie (9 inches)

In a large saucepan, saute onion in butter until tender. Add the soup, turkey, apple, raisins, lemon juice and nutmeg; mix well. Spoon mixture into an ungreased 11-in. x 7-in. x 2-in. baking dish.

On a lightly floured surface, roll out pastry to fit top of dish. Place pastry over filling; flute edges and cut slits in top. Bake potpie at 425° for 25-30 minutes or until crust is golden brown and filling is bubbly. YIELD: 6 SERVINGS.

cooking tip

To flatten chicken breasts for the recipe Light Chicken Cordon Bleu, cover each piece with a piece of plastic wrap and pound from the center out with the flat side of a meat mallet.

sour cream 'n' dill chicken

Sour Cream 'n' Dill Chicken

REBEKAH BROWN • THREE HILLS, ALBERTA

With six children—ages 16 to 6—and frequent guests, it seems I'm always cooking for a crowd. So nearly every recipe I use is doubled or tripled. This chicken entree is an updated version of the Sunday dinner my mother would have prepared. It's the latest favorite with my large, hungry bunch.

PREP: 10 min. **BAKE:** 1 hour

8	to 10 chicken pieces, skinned

Pepper to taste

1	can (10-3/4 ounces) condensed cream of mushroom soup, undiluted
1	envelope dry onion soup mix
1	cup (8 ounces) sour cream
1	tablespoon lemon juice
1	tablespoon fresh dill, chopped *or* 1 teaspoon dill weed
1	can (4 ounces) sliced mushrooms, drained

Paprika
Cooked wide egg noodles, optional

Place chicken in a single layer in a 13-in. x 9-in. x 2-in. baking pan. Sprinkle with pepper. Combine the cream of mushroom soup, soup mix, sour cream, lemon juice, dill and mushrooms; pour over chicken. Sprinkle with paprika.

Bake, uncovered, at 350° for 1 hour or until chicken is tender. Serve over egg noodles if desired. YIELD: 4-6 SERVINGS.

Spinach Turkey Noodle Bake

RAMONA FISH • COLUMBUS, INDIANA

This creamy, comforting bake is a terrific way to use up leftover turkey. I usually freeze diced cooked turkey in 2-cup portions and have them ready to use when someone requests this surprisingly healthy dish.

PREP: 20 min. **BAKE:** 45 min. + standing

2-1/2	cups uncooked yolk-free noodles
2	cups diced cooked turkey breast
1	can (10-3/4 ounces) reduced-fat reduced-sodium condensed cream of chicken soup, undiluted
1/4	teaspoon garlic salt
1/8	teaspoon dried rosemary, crushed

Dash pepper

1	package (10 ounces) frozen chopped spinach, thawed and squeezed dry
1	cup (8 ounces) fat-free cottage cheese
3/4	cup shredded part-skim mozzarella cheese, *divided*
1/8	teaspoon paprika

Cook noodles according to package directions; drain. Meanwhile, in a bowl, combine the turkey, soup, garlic salt, rosemary and pepper. In another bowl, combine the spinach, cottage cheese and 1/2 cup mozzarella cheese.

In a 2-qt. baking dish coated with cooking spray, layer half of the noodles, turkey mixture and cottage cheese mixture. Repeat layers. Cover and bake at 350° for 35 minutes. Uncover; sprinkle with the remaining mozzarella cheese. Bake for 10-15 minutes longer or until edges are lightly browned; sprinkle with paprika. Let casserole stand for 5 minutes before serving. YIELD: 6 SERVINGS.

Turkey Biscuit Potpie

SHIRLEY FRANCEY • ST. CATHARINES, ONTARIO

My family enjoys this classic that is loaded with generous chunks of turkey, potatoes, carrots and green beans. Topped with easy-to-make biscuits, it serves up hearty portions of down-home flavor.

PREP: 30 min. **BAKE:** 20 min.

1	large onion, chopped
1	garlic clove, minced
1-1/2	cups cubed peeled potatoes
1-1/2	cups sliced carrots
1	cup frozen cut green beans, thawed

1	cup reduced-sodium chicken broth
4-1/2	teaspoons all-purpose flour
1	can (10-3/4 ounces) reduced-fat condensed cream of mushroom soup, undiluted
2	cups cubed cooked turkey
2	tablespoons minced fresh parsley
1/2	teaspoon dried basil
1/2	teaspoon dried thyme
1/4	teaspoon pepper

BISCUITS:

1	cup all-purpose flour
2	teaspoons baking powder
1/2	teaspoon dried oregano
2	tablespoons butter
7	tablespoons 1% milk

In a large saucepan coated with cooking spray, cook onion and garlic over medium heat until tender. Add the potatoes, carrots, beans and broth; bring to a boil. Reduce heat; cover and simmer for 15-20 minutes or until potatoes are tender.

Remove from the heat. Combine the flour and mushroom soup; stir into vegetable mixture. Add turkey and seasonings. Transfer to a 2-qt. baking dish coated with cooking spray.

In a large bowl, combine the flour, baking powder and oregano. Cut in the butter until evenly distributed. Stir in milk. Drop batter in six mounds onto hot turkey mixture.

Bake, uncovered, at 400° for 20-25 minutes or until a toothpick inserted in the center of a biscuit comes out clean and biscuits are golden brown.
YIELD: 6 SERVINGS.

Chicken Tortilla Casserole

PAMELA HOEKSTRA • HUDSONVILLE, MICHIGAN

I started making this Southwestern specialty after my husband and I were married. With its zippy flavor, it has been a star on our dinner table ever since.

PREP: 20 min. **BAKE:** 30 min.

1/2	cup chicken broth
1/2	cup chopped onion
1/4	cup chopped celery
3	cups cubed cooked chicken
10	flour tortillas (6 inches), torn into bite-size pieces
1	can (10-3/4 ounces) condensed cream of chicken soup, undiluted
1	can (4 ounces) chopped green chilies
3/4	cup shredded cheddar cheese, *divided*
3/4	cup shredded Monterey Jack cheese, *divided*
1/2	teaspoon white pepper
1	cup salsa

In a saucepan, bring the broth, onion and celery to a boil. Reduce heat; cover and simmer for 5-7 minutes or until vegetables are tender. Place in a large bowl. Add chicken, tortillas, soup, chilies, 1/2 cup cheddar cheese, 1/2 cup Monterey Jack cheese and pepper.

Transfer to a greased 11-in. x 7-in. x 2-in. baking dish. Top with salsa and remaining cheeses. Bake, uncovered, at 350° for 30-35 minutes or until heated through. YIELD: 4-6 SERVINGS.

cooking tip

Not sure what to do with those extra tortillas you didn't use in Chicken Tortilla Casserole? Why not turn them into a quick and tasty snack? Spread one with peanut butter, apple butter and cream cheese and roll it up for an on-the-go snack wrap. Or brush the tortillas with butter, sprinkle with cinnamon-sugar and bake on a cookie sheet until crisp.

chicken tortilla casserole

Baked Pheasant In Gravy

LOU BISHOP • PHILLIPS, WISCONSIN

Pheasant is moist, tender and flavorful prepared this way. Topped with a creamy gravy and sprinkled with crunchy French-fried onions, this entree offers a delicious change from the usual turkey or chicken.

PREP: 15 min. **BAKE:** 45 min.

1/2	cup all-purpose flour
1/2	cup packed brown sugar
6	pheasant *or* grouse breast halves
3	tablespoons butter
1	can (10-3/4 ounces) condensed cream of celery soup, undiluted
1	to 1-1/3 cups water
1	cup chicken broth
1	can (2.8 ounces) French-fried onions

Mashed potatoes *or* hot cooked rice

In a large resealable plastic bag, combine flour and brown sugar; add pheasant pieces, one at time, and shake to coat. In a large skillet over medium heat, brown pheasant on both sides in butter. Transfer to a greased 13-in. x 9-in. x 2-in. baking dish.

Combine soup, water and broth until blended; pour over pheasant. Bake, uncovered, at 350° for 40 minutes. Sprinkle with onions. Bake 5-10 minutes longer or until juices run clear. Serve with potatoes or rice. YIELD: 6 SERVINGS.

chicken veggie casserole

Chicken Veggie Casserole

BONNIE SMITH • GOSHEN, INDIANA

I assemble this delightful and inexpensive one-dish meal often. To save yourself time, you can substitute a package of frozen vegetables if you'd like.

PREP: 10 min. **BAKE:** 1 hour

3	cups cubed cooked chicken
4	medium carrots, cut into chunks
3	medium red potatoes, cut into chunks
3	celery ribs, sliced
1	can (10-3/4 ounces) condensed cream of chicken soup, undiluted
2/3	cup water
1/2	teaspoon salt
1/4	teaspoon pepper

Place chicken in a greased shallow 2-qt. baking dish. Top with the carrots, potatoes and celery. Combine the soup, water, salt and pepper; pour over vegetables.

Cover and bake at 350° for 60-75 minutes or until vegetables are tender. YIELD: 5 SERVINGS.

Cumin Chicken With Apples

RAYMONDE BOURGEOIS • SWASTIKA, ONTARIO

A mixture of onions, apples and mushrooms seasoned with cumin and Worcestershire sauce enhances this tender chicken dish.

PREP: 20 min. **BAKE:** 1 hour

baked pheasant in gravy

4	chicken legs with thighs
2	tablespoons butter
2	medium apples, chopped
2	small onions, halved and sliced
1	can (4-1/2 ounces) mushroom stems and pieces, drained
1	tablespoon all-purpose flour
1	can (10-3/4 ounces) condensed cream of mushroom soup, undiluted
1/2	cup water
1	tablespoon ground cumin
1	teaspoon Worcestershire sauce
3/4	teaspoon salt
1/4	teaspoon pepper
1/4	teaspoon chili powder

Hot cooked rice

In a large skillet, brown chicken in butter. Transfer to a greased 13-in. x 9-in. x 2-in. baking dish. In the drippings, saute the apples, onions and mushrooms until apples are crisp-tender. Stir in the flour, soup, water, cumin, Worcestershire sauce, salt and pepper. Pour over chicken.

Cover and bake at 350° for 1 hour or until the chicken juices run clear. Sprinkle with chili powder. Serve over rice. YIELD: 4 SERVINGS.

turkey noodle stew

In a saucepan, combine remaining ingredients except cheese; cook and stir for 5 minutes or until heated through. Spoon into bread cups; sprinkle with cheese. Bake, uncovered, at 350° for 25-30 minutes or until browned. YIELD: 6 SERVINGS.

Saucy Muffin Cups

KAREN LEHMAN • ABERDEEN, IDAHO

I don't have a lot of extra time on my hands to spend cooking. But after busy days on our dairy farm, everyone expects a good, satisfying supper. To help, I came up with this no-fuss and savory recipe.

PREP: 15 min. **BAKE:** 25 min.

1	loaf (1 pound) frozen bread dough, thawed *or* 12 dinner roll dough portions
2	cups diced cooked chicken
1	can (10-3/4 ounces) condensed cream of mushroom soup, undiluted
1/4	cup sliced ripe olives, drained
1/2	cup sliced frozen carrots, thawed
2	tablespoons minced fresh parsley
1	teaspoon chicken bouillon granules
1/4	teaspoon garlic powder

Dash pepper

1/2	cup shredded sharp cheddar cheese

If using bread dough, punch dough down and divide into 12 pieces. Flatten each piece or roll into a 6-in. circle. Press circles into the bottom and up the sides of greased muffin cups.

Turkey Noodle Stew

TRACI MALONEY • TOMS RIVER, NEW JERSEY

You'll appreciate how easily this hearty stew is to assemble and love the flavor provided by a mixture of turkey, vegetables and noodles. Even if you don't usually go for meal-in-one recipes, you will surprise yourself with this scrumptious skillet entree.

PREP/TOTAL TIME: 30 min.

2	turkey breast tenderloins (about 1/2 pound *each*), cut into 1/4-inch slices
1	medium onion, chopped
1	tablespoon vegetable oil
1	can (14-1/2 ounces) chicken broth
1	can (10-3/4 ounces) condensed cream of celery soup, undiluted
2	cups frozen mixed vegetables
1/2	to 1 teaspoon lemon-pepper seasoning
3	cups uncooked extra-wide egg noodles

In a large skillet, cook turkey and onion in oil for 5-6 minutes or until turkey is no longer pink; drain.

In a large bowl, combine the broth, soup, vegetables and lemon-pepper. Add to the skillet; bring to a boil. Stir in noodles. Reduce heat; cover and simmer for 10 minutes or until noodles and vegetables are tender. YIELD: 6 SERVINGS.

cheddary chicken potpie

and cheddar cheese; blend well. Spoon over hot chicken mixture. Sprinkle with almonds if desired. Bake, uncovered, at 375° for 20-25 minutes or until golden brown. YIELD: 6 SERVINGS.

Turkey Spinach Casserole

BECCA BRANSFIELD • BURNS, TENNESSEE

I lightened up an old family treasure to come up with this turkey, rice and spinach casserole. Accompanied by fresh tomato slices and warm corn bread, this entree is one of my gang's usual requests.

PREP: 20 min. BAKE: 40 min.

1	can (10-3/4 ounces) reduced-fat reduced-sodium condensed cream of chicken soup, undiluted
1/2	cup reduced-fat mayonnaise
1/2	cup water
2	cups cubed cooked turkey breast
1	package (10 ounces) frozen chopped spinach, thawed and squeezed dry
3/4	cup uncooked instant brown rice
1	medium yellow summer squash, cubed
1/4	cup chopped red onion
1	teaspoon ground mustard
1/2	teaspoon dried parsley flakes
1/2	teaspoon garlic powder
1/8	teaspoon pepper
1/4	cup fat-free Parmesan cheese topping
1/8	teaspoon paprika

In a large bowl, combine the soup, mayonnaise and water. Stir in the next nine ingredients. Transfer to a shallow 2-1/2-qt. baking dish coated with cooking spray. Cover and bake at 350° for 35-40 minutes or until rice is tender. Uncover; sprinkle top with Parmesan and paprika. Bake for 5 minutes longer. YIELD: 6 SERVINGS.

Cheddary Chicken Potpie

VICKI RAATZ • WATERLOO, WISCONSIN

This can't-beat chicken bake features a medley of three flavorful cheeses. Some days I make it in the morning so I can just pop it in the oven for dinner or have my husband start baking it if I'm not home.

PREP: 20 min. BAKE: 20 min.

1	can (10-3/4 ounces) condensed cream of chicken soup, undiluted
1	cup milk, *divided*
1/2	cup chopped onion
1	package (3 ounces) cream cheese, softened
1/4	cup chopped celery
1/4	cup shredded carrots
1/4	cup grated Parmesan cheese
1/2	teaspoon salt
3	cups cubed cooked chicken
3	cups frozen chopped broccoli, cooked and drained
1	egg
1	tablespoon vegetable oil
1	cup buttermilk complete pancake mix
1	cup (4 ounces) shredded sharp cheddar cheese
1/4	cup sliced almonds, optional

In a large saucepan, combine soup, 1/2 cup of milk, onion, cream cheese, celery, carrots, Parmesan cheese and salt. Cook and stir until the mixture is hot and cream cheese is melted. Stir in the chicken and broccoli; heat through. Pour into an ungreased 2-qt. baking dish. In a medium bowl, combine the egg, oil and remaining milk. Add the pancake mix

cooking tip

For a brand-new taste, make Turkey Spinach Casserole with cream of mushroom soup or cream of broccoli soup instead. Cubed chicken breast is also a delicious alternative in this versatile recipe.

chicken lasagna

Chicken Lasagna

JANET LORTON • EFFINGHAM, ILLINOIS

When my nephews were younger, I would make their favorite meal for their birthdays...this is what they usually requested. The melted cheese makes it easier for kids to eat their vegetables.

PREP: 20 min. **BAKE:** 35 min. + standing

9	uncooked lasagna noodles
2	cans (10-3/4 ounces *each*) condensed cream of chicken soup, undiluted
2/3	cup milk
2-1/2	cups frozen mixed vegetables
2	cups cubed cooked chicken
18	slices process American cheese

Cook noodles according to package directions; drain. In a large saucepan, combine soup and milk. Cook and stir over low heat until blended. Remove from the heat; stir in vegetables and chicken.

In a greased 13-in. x 9-in. x 2-in. baking dish, layer three noodles, a third of the soup mixture and six cheese slices. Repeat layers twice.

Cover and bake at 350° for 30 minutes. Uncover; bake 5-10 minutes longer or until bubbly. Let stand for 15 minutes before cutting. YIELD: 9-12 SERVINGS.

Spinach Chicken Enchiladas

JOY HEADLEY • GRAND PRAIRIE, TEXAS

My husband is a pastor, so I fix meals for large groups often. This one makes frequent appearances on our table and is a nice change from beef enchiladas.

PREP: 30 min. **BAKE:** 45 min.

4	boneless skinless chicken breast halves, cut into thin strips
1/4	cup chopped onion
1	package (10 ounces) frozen chopped spinach, thawed and well drained
1	can (10-3/4 ounces) condensed cream of mushroom soup, undiluted
3/4	cup milk
1	cup (8 ounces) sour cream
1	teaspoon ground nutmeg
1	teaspoon garlic powder
1	teaspoon onion powder
8	flour tortillas (8 inches)
2	cups (8 ounces) shredded part-skim mozzarella cheese

Minced fresh parsley

Coat a large skillet with cooking spray; cook and stir chicken and onion over medium heat for 6-8 minutes or until chicken is no longer pink. Remove from the heat; add spinach and mix well.

In a bowl, combine soup, milk, sour cream and seasonings; mix well. Stir 3/4 cup into chicken and spinach mixture. Divide evenly among tortillas. Roll up and place, seam side down, in a 13-in. x 9-in. x 2-in. baking pan that has been sprayed with cooking spray. Pour the remaining soup mixture over the enchiladas.

Cover and bake at 350° for 30 minutes. Uncover and sprinkle with cheese; return to the oven for 15 minutes or until cheese is melted and bubbly. Garnish with parsley. YIELD: 8 SERVINGS.

spinach chicken enchiladas

Turkey Tetrazzini

SUSAN PAYNE • CORNER BROOK, NEWFOUNDLAND

I make this recipe with leftover turkey, and it's a whole new meal! We look forward to having it after Christmas and Thanksgiving and other times when I roast a turkey for a family gathering.

PREP: 25 min. **BAKE:** 25 min.

1	package (7 ounces) thin spaghetti, broken in half
2	cups cubed cooked turkey
1	cup sliced fresh mushrooms
1	small onion, chopped
3	tablespoons butter, melted
1	can (10-3/4 ounces) condensed cream of mushroom soup, undiluted
1	cup milk
1/2	teaspoon poultry seasoning
1/8	teaspoon ground mustard
1	cup (4 ounces) shredded cheddar cheese
1	cup (4 ounces) shredded part-skim mozzarella cheese
1	tablespoon shredded Parmesan cheese

Minced fresh parsley

Cook spaghetti according to package directions. Drain and place in a greased 11-in. x 7-in. x 2-in. baking dish. Top with turkey; set aside.

In a large skillet, saute the mushrooms and onion in butter until tender. Whisk in the soup, milk,

chicken in a cloud

poultry seasoning and mustard until blended. Stir in cheddar cheese. Cook and stir over medium heat until cheese is melted. Pour over turkey.

Sprinkle with cheeses (dish will be full). Bake, uncovered, at 350° for 25-30 minutes or until heated through and cheese is melted. Sprinkle with parsley. YIELD: 4-6 SERVINGS.

Chicken in a Cloud

MRS. ROBERT LAWER • ISHPEMING, MICHIGAN

I enjoy this tasty dish with a garden salad, corn on the cob and a warm dinner roll. The greatest thing about casseroles like this one—besides eating them—is that they can be prepared ahead of time. This recipe is perfect for hearty appetites.

PREP: 15 min. **BAKE:** 40 min.

POTATO SHELL:

3-1/2	cups mashed potatoes (no milk, butter *or* seasoning added)
1-1/2	cups (6 ounces) shredded cheddar cheese
1	can (2.8 ounces) French-fried onions
2	tablespoons chopped fresh parsley

Salt to taste

FILLING:

1-1/2	cups shredded *or* cubed cooked chicken *or* turkey
1	package (10 ounces) frozen mixed vegetables, thawed and drained
1	can (10-3/4 ounces) condensed cream of chicken soup, undiluted

turkey tetrazzini

1/4 cup milk
1/2 teaspoon ground mustard
1/4 teaspoon garlic powder
1/4 teaspoon pepper

Combine all of the potato shell ingredients; spread over the bottom and up the sides of a greased 2-qt. shallow baking dish. In a large bowl, combine filling ingredients; pour gently into shell.

Bake, uncovered, at 375° for 40 minutes or until heated through. Let casserole stand for 5 minutes before serving. YIELD: 6-8 SERVINGS.

Chicken & Ham Roll-Ups

KAREN MAWHINNEY • TEESEWATER, ONTARIO

I first started making these easy roll-ups as a way to use leftover chicken. My family raved about them so much that I now frequently serve them during the week and when we entertain guests.

PREP/TOTAL TIME: 30 min.

3 cups cooked rice
1-1/2 cups chopped cooked chicken
1 can (10-3/4 ounces) condensed cream of chicken soup, undiluted, *divided*
1/4 cup finely chopped celery
1 green onion, thinly sliced
1/4 teaspoon pepper, *divided*
6 slices fully cooked ham
1/4 cup sour cream *or* plain yogurt
1/4 cup milk
1/4 teaspoon dried thyme
1/2 cup shredded Swiss *or* part-skim mozzarella cheese
Paprika *or* additional chopped green onion

Spread rice in a greased 11-in. x 7-in. x 2-in. microwave-safe baking dish; set aside. In a medium bowl, combine chicken, 1/3 cup soup, celery, onion and 1/8 teaspoon pepper. Place 1/4 cup on each ham slice and roll up. Secure with a toothpick if necessary. Place ham rolls, seam side down, on top of rice.

Combine sour cream, milk, thyme and remaining soup and pepper; spoon over rolls. Cover and microwave on high, turning dish halfway through cooking time, for 6-10 minutes or until heated through. Sprinkle with cheese and paprika or onion; cover and let stand 5 minutes. Remove toothpicks before serving. YIELD: 4-6 SERVINGS.

EDITOR'S NOTE: This recipe was tested in a 1,100-watt microwave.

lemon-curry chicken casserole

Lemon-Curry Chicken Casserole

SUE YAEGER • BROOKINGS, SOUTH DAKOTA

Asparagus and almonds add a flavorful twist to an ordinary chicken hot bake. I've made it countless times for company and am usually asked for the recipe.

PREP: 20 min. **BAKE:** 40 min.

2 packages (12 ounces *each*) frozen cut asparagus, thawed and drained
4 boneless skinless chicken breast halves, cut into 1/2-inch strips
Salt and pepper to taste
3 tablespoons butter
1 can (10-3/4 ounces) condensed cream of chicken soup, undiluted
1/2 cup mayonnaise
1/4 cup lemon juice
1 teaspoon curry powder
1/4 teaspoon ground ginger
1/8 teaspoon pepper
1/2 cup sliced almonds, toasted

Place asparagus in a greased 11-in. x 7-in. x 2-in. baking dish; set aside. Sprinkle chicken with salt and pepper.

In a large skillet, saute chicken in butter for 10-14 minutes or until juices run clear. Place over asparagus. Combine soup, mayonnaise, lemon juice, curry powder, ginger and pepper; spoon over chicken.

Bake, uncovered, at 350° for 35 minutes. Sprinkle with almonds and return to the oven for 5 minutes. YIELD: 6 SERVINGS.

chicken saltimbocca

Chicken Saltimbocca

CAROL MCCOLLOUGH • MISSOULA, MONTANA

White wine dresses up cream of chicken soup to make a lovely sauce for chicken, ham and Swiss cheese roll-ups. The tried-and-true recipe comes from my mother.

PREP: 25 min. + chilling **COOK:** 4 hours

6	boneless skinless chicken breast halves
6	thin slices deli ham
6	slices Swiss cheese
1/4	cup all-purpose flour
1/4	cup grated Parmesan cheese
1/2	teaspoon salt
1/4	teaspoon pepper
2	tablespoons vegetable oil
1	can (10-3/4 ounces) condensed cream of chicken soup, undiluted
1/2	cup dry white wine *or* chicken broth

Hot cooked rice

Flatten chicken to 1/4-in. thickness. Top each piece with a slice of ham and cheese. Roll up tightly; secure with toothpicks. In a shallow bowl, combine the flour, Parmesan cheese, salt and pepper. Roll chicken in flour mixture; refrigerate for 1 hour.

In a skillet, brown roll-ups in oil on all sides; transfer to a 3-qt. slow cooker. Combine the soup and wine or broth; pour over chicken. Cover and cook on low for 4-5 hours or until a meat thermometer reads 170°. Remove roll-ups and stir sauce. Serve with rice. YIELD: 6 SERVINGS.

Asparagus Supreme

BETTY TEEGARDEN • POLO, MISSOURI

My husband and I enjoy spending time in the kitchen and trying new recipes. It's fun to create new dishes—especially when they're as successful as this one.

PREP: 15 min. **BAKE:** 40 min.

3	cups cooked rice
1	teaspoon salt, *divided*
3/4	teaspoon pepper, *divided*
1	package (12 ounces) frozen cut asparagus, thawed and drained
4	boneless skinless chicken breast halves, cut into 1-inch strips
1/4	cup vegetable oil
1	cup sliced fresh mushrooms
6	green onions, chopped
1/4	cup chopped sweet red pepper
1	can (10-3/4 ounces) condensed cream of mushroom soup, undiluted
1/2	cup mayonnaise
2	teaspoons lemon juice
1	teaspoon salt-free seasoning blend
1/2	cup shredded cheddar cheese

Spread rice in a greased 11-in. x 7-in. x 2-in. baking dish. Sprinkle rice with 1/2 teaspoon salt and 1/4 teaspoon pepper. Cover with asparagus. Sprinkle chicken with remaining salt and pepper. In a large skillet, cook chicken in oil over medium-high heat until browned on all sides. With a slotted spoon, remove chicken and place over asparagus. Add mushrooms, onions and red pepper to skillet; saute until tender. Spoon over chicken. Combine soup, mayonnaise, lemon juice and seasoning blend; spread over vegetables. Sprinkle with cheese. Cover and bake at 350° for 40-45 minutes. YIELD: 6 SERVINGS.

Creamy Chicken & Broccoli

TAMARA KALSBEEK • GRAND RAPIDS, MICHIGAN

My gang likes the taste of chicken cordon bleu, but I don't like the time required to make it. This skillet sensation, with the addition of broccoli, gives my family the flavors they crave with only a fraction of the work.

PREP/TOTAL TIME: 30 min.

1	pound boneless skinless chicken breasts, cut into 1-inch cubes

1 small onion, chopped
2 tablespoons butter
1 can (10-3/4 ounces) condensed cream
   of mushroom soup, undiluted
2/3 cup mayonnaise
1/2 cup sour cream
2 tablespoons white wine *or* chicken
   broth
1/8 teaspoon garlic powder
Salt and pepper to taste
1 cup cubed fully cooked ham
1 package (10 ounces) frozen broccoli
   florets, thawed
3 bacon strips, cooked and crumbled
Hot cooked pasta *or* rice
1 cup (4 ounces) shredded Swiss cheese,
   optional

In a large skillet, saute chicken and onion in butter until meat is no longer pink.

Meanwhile, in a large bowl, combine the soup, mayonnaise, sour cream, wine or broth, garlic powder, salt and pepper. Add to the chicken mixture.

Stir in the ham, broccoli and bacon; cover and cook until heated through. Serve over pasta; sprinkle with cheese if desired. YIELD: 4 SERVINGS.

EDITOR'S NOTE: Reduced-fat or fat-free mayonnaise is not recommended for this recipe.

cooking tip

When cutting the chicken breasts into strips for Asparagus Supreme, you'll want to make the strips of uniform size. To do this easily, cut the chicken before it is completely thawed. Using a kitchen shears instead of a knife will also make it easier to cut into strips. After you handle raw chicken, make sure to wash the cutting board, countertop, scissors and your hands thoroughly with hot, soapy water.

Swiss Chicken

ELIZABETH MONTGOMERY,
CAMBRIDGE, MASSACHUSETTS

I like to impress our guests with this palate-pleasing chicken topped with stuffing and Swiss cheese. I usually serve it with corn and a salad, since the stuffing is a side dish in itself.

PREP: 5 min. **BAKE:** 1 hour

6 boneless skinless chicken breast
   halves (4 ounces *each*)
1 cup (4 ounces) shredded Swiss cheese
5 cups seasoned stuffing mix
1 can (10-3/4 ounces) condensed cream
   of mushroom soup, undiluted
1 cup (8 ounces) sour cream

Place chicken in a greased 13-in. x 9-in. x 2-in. baking dish; sprinkle with shredded Swiss cheese and stuffing mix. Combine cream of mushroom soup and sour cream; spread soup mixture over stuffing. Bake, uncovered, at 375° for 1 hour or until the meat juices run clear. YIELD: 6 SERVINGS.

Tasty Turkey Casserole

MAUREEN DONGOSKI • PETERSBURG, WEST VIRGINIA

A can of cream soup makes it easy to assemble this crowd-pleasing casserole. Sour cream adds a rich taste to the sauce. I highly recommend bringing this to your next bring-a-dish event.

PREP: 20 min. **BAKE:** 20 min.

6 cups fresh broccoli florets
1 cup water
6 cups cubed cooked turkey breast
1 can (10-3/4 ounces) condensed cream
   of chicken soup, undiluted
1 cup (8 ounces) sour cream
3/4 cup shredded Swiss cheese

In a large saucepan, combine the broccoli and water. Bring to a boil. Reduce heat. Cover and simmer for 6-8 minutes or until crisp-tender; drain. Transfer to a 13-in. x 9-in. x 2-in. baking dish coated with cooking spray. Sprinkle with turkey.

Combine the cream of chicken soup and sour cream. Spoon soup mixture over the turkey. Sprinkle with shredded Swiss cheese. Bake, uncovered, at 375° for 20-25 minutes or until heated through. YIELD: 10 SERVINGS.

CHAPTER 7
Seafood

Salmon Macaroni Bake

CARRIE MITCHELL • RALEIGH, NORTH CAROLINA

A neighbor brought us this creamy casserole the night after our newborn daughter came home from the hospital. It was so good, we couldn't resist heating up the leftovers for breakfast the next morning.

PREP: 20 min. **BAKE:** 30 min.

- 1 package (14 ounces) deluxe macaroni and cheese dinner mix
- 1 can (10-3/4 ounces) condensed cream of mushroom soup, undiluted
- 1/2 cup milk
- 1 can (6 ounces) boneless skinless salmon, drained
- 1 tablespoon grated onion *or* 1/2 teaspoon onion powder
- 1/2 cup shredded cheddar cheese
- 1/2 cup dry bread crumbs
- 2 tablespoons butter, cubed

Prepare macaroni and cheese according to package directions. Stir in the soup, milk, salmon, onion and cheddar cheese. Transfer to a greased 1-1/2-qt. baking dish. Sprinkle top with bread crumbs; dot with butter. Bake, uncovered, at 375° for 30 minutes or until heated through. YIELD: 4 SERVINGS.

Tuna Patties

SONYA SHERRILL • SIOUX CITY, IOWA

My family likes anything that features stuffing mix, so these tuna burgers are a popular request. I need only minutes to form the moist patties, brown them in a skillet and mix up the swift sauce to serve on the side.

PREP/TOTAL TIME: 30 min.

- 2 eggs, lightly beaten
- 1 can (10-3/4 ounces) condensed cream of mushroom soup, undiluted, *divided*
- 3/4 cup milk, *divided*
- 2 cups stuffing mix
- 1 can (12 ounces) tuna, drained and flaked
- 2 tablespoons butter

In a large bowl, combine the eggs, a third of the soup and 1/4 cup milk. Stir in stuffing mix and tuna. Shape into eight patties.

In a large skillet, brown patties in butter for 3-4 minutes on each side or until heated through. Meanwhile, in a small saucepan, heat remaining soup and milk. Serve with patties. YIELD: 4 SERVINGS.

crab alfredo

Crab Alfredo

SUSAN ANSTINE • YORK, PENNSYLVANIA

Canned soup and sour cream speed along a rich sauce that coats imitation crab. When spooned over tender penne pasta and garnished with grated Parmesan cheese and fresh parsley, it's a quick-to-fix entree that looks and tastes elegant.

PREP/TOTAL TIME: 25 min.

- 1 package (16 ounces) penne pasta
- 1/2 cup chopped onion
- 1/4 cup butter
- 2 cups (16 ounces) sour cream
- 1 can (10-3/4 ounces) condensed cream of mushroom soup, undiluted
- 1/2 cup milk
- 1/2 teaspoon salt
- 1/2 teaspoon garlic powder
- 1/2 teaspoon Italian seasoning
- 1/4 teaspoon pepper
- 2 packages (8 ounces *each*) imitation crabmeat, flaked
- 1/4 cup grated Parmesan cheese
- 2 tablespoons minced fresh parsley

Cook pasta according to package directions.

Meanwhile, in a large skillet, saute onion in butter until tender. Whisk in the sour cream, soup, milk, salt, garlic powder, Italian seasoning and pepper until blended. Cook and stir until heated through (do not boil). Stir in crab; heat through.

Drain pasta; top with crab sauce. Sprinkle with Parmesan cheese and parsley. YIELD: 8 SERVINGS.

onions neptune

Onions Neptune

TODD NOON • GALLOWAY, NEW JERSEY

I serve this dish often and usually add whatever ingredients I have on hand, such as sliced mushrooms or sun-dried tomatoes. Whether I serve it "as is" or jazz it up, it is always delicious.

PREP: 20 min. BAKE: 35 min.

5	to 6 medium sweet onions, sliced and separated into rings
1/2	cup butter, softened, *divided*
2	cans (6 ounces each) lump crabmeat, drained, *divided*
3	cups (12 ounces) shredded Swiss cheese
1	can (10-3/4 ounces) condensed cream of mushroom soup, undiluted
1/2	cup evaporated milk
1/2	teaspoon salt
1/4	teaspoon pepper
12	to 16 slices French bread (1/4 inch thick)

In a large skillet, saute onions in 1/4 cup butter until tender. Remove from the heat; gently stir in half of the crab. Spread into a greased 13-in. x 9-in. x 2-in. baking dish. Top with remaining crab. Combine the cheese, soup, milk, salt and pepper; spoon mixture over the crab.

Spread remaining butter over one side of each slice of bread; place buttered side up over casserole. Bake, uncovered, at 350° for 35-45 minutes or until golden brown. YIELD: 12 SERVINGS.

Cheesy Tuna Lasagna

VIRGINIA FERRIS • LYONS, MICHIGAN

This wonderful bake was added to my recipe collection many years ago. The tuna and three-cheese blend wins over doubters who say they aren't fond of fish.

PREP: 15 min. BAKE: 25 min. + standing

1	medium onion, chopped
2	tablespoons butter
1	can (12 ounces) tuna, drained and flaked
1	can (10-3/4 ounces) condensed cream of mushroom soup, undiluted
1/2	cup milk
1/2	teaspoon garlic salt
1/2	teaspoon dried oregano
1/4	teaspoon pepper
9	lasagna noodles, cooked and drained
1-1/2	cups (12 ounces) 4% cottage cheese
8	ounces sliced part-skim mozzarella cheese
1/4	cup grated Parmesan cheese

In a large saucepan, saute onion in butter until tender. Stir in the tuna, soup, milk, garlic salt, oregano and pepper until combined. Spread 3/4 cupful into a greased 11-in. x 7-in. x 2-in. baking dish.

Layer with three noodles (trimming if necessary), 3/4 cup tuna mixture, half of the cottage cheese and a third of the mozzarella cheese. Repeat layers. Top with remaining noodles, tuna mixture and mozzarella. Sprinkle with Parmesan cheese.

Bake, uncovered, at 350° for 25-30 minutes or until bubbly. Let stand for 10-15 minutes before serving. YIELD: 6-8 SERVINGS.

Blend of the Bayou

RUBY WILLIAMS • BOGALUSA, LOUISIANA

My sister-in-law shared this seafood medley when I first moved to Louisiana. It's been handed down in my husband's family for generations. It is quick to prepare, nutritious and requested frequently.

PREP: 20 min. BAKE: 25 min.

1	package (8 ounces) cream cheese, cubed
4	tablespoons butter, *divided*
1	large onion, chopped
2	celery ribs, chopped
1	large green pepper, chopped
1	pound cooked medium shrimp, peeled and deveined

2 cans (6 ounces *each*) crabmeat,
drained, flaked and cartilage removed
1 can (10-3/4 ounces) condensed cream
of mushroom soup, undiluted
3/4 cup cooked rice
1 jar (4-1/2 ounces) sliced mushrooms,
drained
1 teaspoon garlic salt
3/4 teaspoon hot pepper sauce
1/2 teaspoon cayenne pepper
3/4 cup shredded cheddar cheese
1/2 cup crushed butter-flavored crackers
(about 12 crackers)

In a small saucepan, cook and stir the cream cheese and 2 tablespoons butter over low heat until melted and smooth; set aside.

In a large skillet, saute the onion, celery and green pepper in remaining butter until tender. Stir in the shrimp, crab, soup, rice, mushrooms, garlic salt, pepper sauce, cayenne and reserved cream cheese mixture.

Transfer to a greased 2-qt. baking dish. Combine cheddar cheese and cracker crumbs; sprinkle over the top. Bake, uncovered, at 350° for 25-30 minutes or until bubbly. YIELD: 6-8 SERVINGS.

Special Seafood Linguine

VALERIE PUTSEY • WINAMAC, INDIANA

When entertaining, I like to rely on this hearty pasta entree. To avoid some last-minute fuss, I choose to chop the onion and green pepper, and peel and devein the shrimp earlier in the day.

PREP: 10 min. COOK: 35 min.

1 large red onion, chopped
1/2 cup chopped green pepper
3 garlic cloves, minced
1/3 cup minced fresh parsley
1/4 cup olive oil
1 can (28 ounces) diced tomatoes,
undrained
1 can (10-3/4 ounces) condensed cream
of shrimp soup, undiluted
1 tablespoon lemon juice
1 teaspoon dried basil
1 teaspoon dried oregano
1/4 teaspoon salt
1/4 teaspoon pepper
1 pound uncooked medium shrimp,
peeled and deveined

2 cans (6 ounces *each*) crabmeat,
drained, flaked and cartilage removed
1 package (16 ounces) linguine
1/4 cup shredded Parmesan cheese

In a large skillet, saute the onion, green pepper, garlic and parsley in oil until tender. Add the tomatoes, soup, lemon juice and seasonings. Bring to a boil. Reduce heat; simmer, uncovered, for 20 minutes.

Stir in the shrimp and crab; simmer for 10 minutes or until shrimp turn pink. Meanwhile, cook the linguine according to package directions; drain. Serve seafood mixture over linguine; sprinkle with Parmesan cheese. YIELD: 6-8 SERVINGS.

Shrimp Newburg

DONNA SOUDERS • HAGERSTOWN, MARYLAND

A friend gave me the recipe for this tasty time-saver that takes advantage of cooked shrimp. It's a no-fuss company meal when served over rice and accompanied by a tossed salad and dessert.

PREP/TOTAL TIME: 15 min.

1 can (10-3/4 ounces) condensed cream
of shrimp *or* mushroom soup, undiluted
1/4 cup water
1 teaspoon seafood seasoning
1 package (1 pound) frozen cooked
medium salad shrimp, thawed
Hot cooked rice

In a saucepan, combine the soup, water and seafood seasoning. Bring to boil. Reduce heat; stir in shrimp. Heat through. Serve shrimp mixture over rice. YIELD: 4 SERVINGS.

shrimp newburg

Creamy Seafood Enchiladas

EVELYN GEBHARDT • KASILOF, ALASKA

A shrimp and crab combo and a flavorful sauce make this variation on a Mexican favorite outstanding. I prepare them for an annual fund-raiser, where they're always in demand. Spice up the recipe by adding more green chilies and salsa.

PREP: 20 min. **BAKE:** 30 min.

1/4	cup butter
1/4	cup all-purpose flour
1	cup chicken broth
1	can (10-3/4 ounces) condensed cream of chicken soup, undiluted
1	cup (8 ounces) sour cream
1/2	cup salsa
1/8	teaspoon salt
1	cup (8 ounces) 4% cottage cheese
1	pound small shrimp, cooked, peeled and deveined
1	cup cooked *or* canned crabmeat, drained, flaked and cartilage removed
1-1/2	cups (6 ounces) shredded Monterey Jack cheese
1	can (4 ounces) chopped green chilies
1	tablespoon dried cilantro *or* parsley flakes
12	flour tortillas (7 inches)
	Additional salsa

In a saucepan over low heat, melt butter; stir in flour until smooth. Gradually stir in broth and soup until blended. Bring to a boil; cook and stir for 2 minutes or until slightly thickened. Remove from the heat. Stir in sour cream, salsa and salt; set aside.

Place the cottage cheese in a blender; cover and process until smooth. Transfer cottage cheese to a bowl; add the shrimp, crab, Monterey Jack cheese, green chilies and cilantro.

Spread 3/4 cup sauce in a greased 13-in. x 9-in. x 2-in. baking dish. Place about 1/3 cup seafood mixture down the center of each tortilla. Roll up and place seam side down over sauce. Top with the remaining sauce. Bake, uncovered, at 350° for 30-35 minutes or until heated through. Serve with additional salsa. YIELD: 6 SERVINGS.

creamy seafood enchiladas

Broccoli Tuna Roll-Ups

JENNA LEE GARRETT • NORMAN, OKLAHOMA

It's easy to enjoy your guests when you have this main dish on the menu. It's one you can make ahead and then warm up as you mingle. I often take this as a "dish to pass" and it's a rave-winner every time!

PREP: 10 min. **BAKE:** 35 min.

1	can (10-3/4 ounces) condensed cream of mushroom soup, undiluted
1	cup milk
1	can (12-1/2 ounces) tuna, drained and flaked
2-1/2	cups broccoli florets, cooked
1	cup (4 ounces) shredded cheddar cheese, *divided*
1	can (2.8 ounces) French-fried onions, *divided*
6	small flour tortillas (6 to 7 inches)
1/2	cup chopped tomatoes, optional

In a small bowl, combine soup and milk; set aside. In a medium bowl, combine tuna, broccoli, 1/2 cup cheddar cheese, half of the onions and 3/4 cup of the soup mixture; mix well. Divide mixture among the tortillas and roll up.

Place, seam side down, in a greased 12-in. x 8-in. x 2-in. baking dish. Pour remaining soup mixture over tortillas. Sprinkle with tomatoes if desired.

Cover and bake at 350° for 35 minutes. Uncover; sprinkle with remaining cheese and onions. Return to the oven for 5 minutes. YIELD: 3-6 SERVINGS.

Salmon Supper

DEBRA KNIPPEL • MEDFORD, WISCONSIN

With a husband and four children to cook for, I'm always on the lookout for swift recipes. This one was given to me many years ago by my mother-in-law. In addition to being very quick to fix, it's a favorite family comfort food.

PREP/TOTAL TIME: 30 min.

1/3	cup chopped green pepper
3	tablespoons chopped onion
2	tablespoons vegetable oil
1/4	cup all-purpose flour
1/2	teaspoon salt
1-1/2	cups milk
1	can (10-3/4 ounces) condensed cream of celery soup, undiluted
2	pouches (3 ounces *each*) boneless skinless pink salmon
1	cup frozen peas
2	teaspoons lemon juice
1	tube (8 ounces) refrigerated crescent rolls

In a large skillet, saute green pepper and onion in oil for 3-4 minutes or until crisp-tender.

In a small bowl, combine flour, salt, milk and soup until blended. Add to the skillet. Bring to a boil. Reduce heat; cook and stir for 2 minutes or until smooth. Stir in the salmon, peas and lemon juice.

Pour into an ungreased 11-in. x 7-in. x 2-in. baking dish. Do not unroll crescent dough; cut into eight equal slices. Arrange over salmon mixture. Bake, uncovered, at 375° for 10-12 minutes or until golden brown. YIELD: 4 SERVINGS.

Stuffed Sole

WINNIE HIGGINS • SALISBURY, MARYLAND

Seafood was a staple for my large family when I was growing up. Inspired by my mother's incredible meals, I developed this entree. The fish is moist and flavorful, and the sauce is so good over rice.

PREP: 20 min. **BAKE:** 35 min.

1	cup chopped onion
2	cans (6 ounces *each*) small shrimp, rinsed and drained
1	jar (4-1/2 ounces) sliced mushrooms, drained
2	tablespoons butter
1/2	pound fresh cooked *or* canned crabmeat, drained and cartilage removed

stuffed sole

8	sole *or* flounder fillets (2 to 2-1/2 pounds)
1/2	teaspoon salt
1/4	teaspoon pepper
1/4	teaspoon paprika
2	cans (10-3/4 ounces *each*) condensed cream of mushroom soup, undiluted
1/3	cup chicken broth
2	tablespoons water
2/3	cup shredded cheddar cheese
2	tablespoons minced fresh parsley
	Cooked wild, brown *or* white rice *or* a mixture, optional

In a saucepan, saute onion, shrimp and mushrooms in butter until onion is tender. Add crabmeat; heat through. Sprinkle flounder fillets with salt, pepper and paprika. Spoon crabmeat mixture on fillets; roll up and fasten with a toothpick.

Place in a greased 13-in. x 9-in. x 2-in. baking dish. Combine the soup, broth and water; blend until smooth. Pour over fillets. Sprinkle with cheese. Cover and bake at 400° for 30 minutes. Sprinkle with parsley; return to the oven, uncovered, for 5 minutes or until the fish flakes easily with a fork. Serve over rice if desired. YIELD: 8 SERVINGS.

cooking tip

When buying fresh fish, such as sole or flounder fillets used in Stuffed Sole, look for firm fish that is elastic to the touch, is moist looking and has a mild aroma.

wild rice shrimp bake

Curried Shrimp

SUE FRIEND • LYNDEN, WASHINGTON

If you like curry, you'll enjoy the rich flavor found in this spicy shrimp mixture. It's wonderful served over hot rice. I like to garnish it with bacon bits and chopped hard-cooked eggs.

PREP/TOTAL TIME: 15 min.

1   small onion, chopped
1   tablespoon vegetable oil
1   can (10-3/4 ounces) condensed cream of shrimp soup, undiluted
1   teaspoon curry powder
1   package (1 pound) frozen uncooked small shrimp, thawed, peeled and deveined
1   cup (8 ounces) sour cream
Hot cooked rice

In a large saucepan, saute onion in oil until tender. Stir in soup and curry powder; bring to a boil. Add the shrimp; cook and stir until shrimp turn pink. Reduce heat. Stir in sour cream; heat through. Serve over rice. YIELD: 4 SERVINGS.

Wild Rice Shrimp Bake

LEE STEARNS • MOBILE, ALABAMA

Fresh shrimp lends a special touch to this effortless entree that starts out with a boxed wild rice mix. I like to top off the creamy meal-in-one with a handful of crunchy, seasoned croutons.

PREP: 20 min. **BAKE:** 20 min.

1   package (6 ounces) long grain and wild rice mix
1   pound uncooked medium shrimp, peeled and deveined
1   medium green pepper, chopped
1   medium onion, chopped
1   can (4 ounces) mushroom stems and pieces, drained
1/4   cup butter
1   can (10-3/4 ounces) condensed cream of chicken soup, undiluted
1/2   cup seasoned stuffing croutons

Prepare rice according to package directions.

Meanwhile, in a large skillet, saute the shrimp, green pepper, onion and mushrooms in butter until shrimp turn pink. Add the soup to the rice; stir into the shrimp mixture.

Transfer to a greased 2-qt. baking dish. Sprinkle with croutons. Bake, uncovered, at 350° for 20-25 minutes or until heated through. YIELD: 6 SERVINGS.

Corn Bread-Topped Salmon

BILLIE WILSON • MASONIC HOME, KENTUCKY

There's no need to serve bread when you've already baked it into your main dish. This economical casserole tastes great with tuna or chicken as well.

PREP: 15 min. **BAKE:** 30 min.

2   cans (10-3/4 ounces *each*) condensed cream of mushroom soup, undiluted
1/4   cup milk
1   can (14-3/4 ounces) salmon, drained, bones and skin removed
1-1/2 cups frozen peas, thawed
1   package (8-1/2 ounces) corn bread/muffin mix
1   jar (4 ounces) diced pimientos, drained
1/4   cup finely chopped green pepper
1   teaspoon finely chopped onion
1/2   teaspoon celery seed
1/4   teaspoon dried thyme

In a large saucepan, bring soup and milk to a boil; add salmon and peas. Pour into a greased shallow 2-1/2-qt. baking dish. Prepare corn bread batter according to package direction; stir in the remaining ingredients. Spoon over salmon mixture.

Bake, uncovered, at 400° for 30-35 minutes or until a toothpick inserted in the corn bread comes out clean. YIELD: 6-8 SERVINGS.

Quick Crab Mornay

GENEVA SCHMIDTKA • CANANDAIGUA, NEW YORK

This luscious, cheesy sauce is a wonderful way to show-case canned crab meat. The elegant mixture can be served with toast for a special lunch or over chicken, rice or potatoes for a distinctive dinner.

PREP/TOTAL TIME: 30 min.

1	can (10-3/4 ounces) condensed cream of chicken soup, undiluted
1/3	cup white wine *or* chicken broth
1	egg, lightly beaten
1	can (6 ounces) crabmeat, drained, flaked and cartilage removed
1/2	cup shredded cheddar cheese

In a small saucepan, combine soup and wine or broth. Cook and stir over medium heat until blended and heated through. Stir 1/2 cupful into the egg; return all to the pan.

Place the crab in a greased shallow 1-qt. baking dish; top with soup mixture. Sprinkle with cheese. Bake, uncovered, at 350° for 20 minutes or until the top is lightly browned and cheese is melted. YIELD: 4-6 SERVINGS.

cooking tip

Salmon in 12-ounce cans has already been boned and skinned, while salmon in 14-3/4-ounce cans has not. If the recipe you're using calls for the larger can of salmon, but you want to save yourself the trouble of removing the bones and skin, buy two of the smaller ones and use the extra fish to make salmon cakes the next day.

Tuna in the Straw Casserole

KALLEE MCCREERY • ESCONDIDO, CALIFORNIA

Shoestring potatoes make this family-pleaser a winner in my house. Even my husband, who doesn't normally care for tuna, counts it among his favorites.

PREP/TOTAL TIME: 30 min.

1	can (10-3/4 ounces) condensed cream of mushroom soup, undiluted
1	can (5 ounces) evaporated milk
1	can (6 ounces) tuna, drained and flaked
1	can (4 ounces) mushroom stems and pieces, drained
1	cup frozen mixed vegetables, thawed
2	cups potato sticks, *divided*

In a large bowl, combine the soup and milk until blended. Stir in the tuna, mushrooms, vegetables and 1-1/2 cups potato sticks.

Transfer to a greased 1-1/2-qt. baking dish. Bake, uncovered, at 375° for 20 minutes. Sprinkle with remaining potato sticks. Bake 5-10 minutes longer or until bubbly and potatoes are crisp. YIELD: 4 SERVINGS.

tuna in the straw casserole

Catch-of-the-Day Casserole

CATHY CLUGSTON • CLOVERDALE, INDIANA

This super salmon recipe comes from my mother-in-law. She is one of the best cooks I know and one of the best mothers—a real gem.

PREP: 15 min. **BAKE:** 30 min.

4	ounces uncooked small shell pasta
1	can (10-3/4 ounces) condensed cream of celery soup, undiluted
1/2	cup mayonnaise
1/4	cup milk
1/4	cup shredded cheddar cheese
1	package (10 ounces) frozen peas, thawed
1	can (7-1/2 ounces) salmon, drained, bones and skin removed
1	tablespoon finely chopped onion

Cook pasta according to package directions. Meanwhile, in a large bowl, combine the soup, mayonnaise, milk and cheese until blended. Stir in the peas, salmon and chopped onion.

Drain pasta; add to salmon mixture. Transfer to a greased 2-qt. baking dish. Bake casserole, uncovered, at 350° for 30-35 minutes or until bubbly. YIELD: 4 SERVINGS.

EDITOR'S NOTE: Reduced-fat or fat-free mayonnaise is not recommended for this recipe.

catch-of-the-day casserole

Hurry-Up Tuna Supper

DOROTHY PRITCHETT • WILLS POINT, TEXAS

A variety of convenience products, including canned tuna, frozen vegetables and instant rice, are used to prepare this no-fuss, satisfying supper.

PREP/TOTAL TIME: 15 min.

1	package (10 ounces) frozen mixed vegetables
2	cups water
2	tablespoons dried minced onion
1/2	teaspoon salt
1	can (10-3/4 ounces) condensed cream of celery soup, undiluted
1-1/3	cups uncooked instant rice
1	can (6 ounces) tuna, drained and flaked
2	teaspoons dried parsley flakes
3/4	teaspoon dried marjoram
1	teaspoon lemon juice

In a skillet, combine the vegetables, water, onion and salt. Bring to a boil over medium heat. Stir in the soup, rice, tuna, parsley and marjoram. Reduce heat; cover and simmer for 5-10 minutes or until the rice is tender and the liquid is absorbed. Stir in lemon juice. Serve immediately. YIELD: 4 SERVINGS.

Crumb-Topped Haddock

DEBBIE SOLT • LEWISTOWN, PENNSYLVANIA

With only five ingredients, this scrumptious dish with a crispy topping is a breeze to make. It's the perfect time-saver when nights are busy or the pantry is looking bare!

PREP: 5 min. **BAKE:** 35 min.

2	pounds haddock *or* cod fillets
1	can (10-3/4 ounces) condensed cream of shrimp soup, undiluted
1	teaspoon grated onion
1	teaspoon Worcestershire sauce
1	cup crushed butter-flavored crackers (about 25 crackers)

Arrange fillets in a greased 13-in. x 9-in. x 2-in. baking dish. Combine the cream of shrimp soup, onion and Worcestershire sauce; pour over fish.

Bake, uncovered, at 375° for 20 minutes. Sprinkle fish with cracker crumbs. Bake 15 minutes longer or until the fish flakes easily with a fork. YIELD: 6-8 SERVINGS.

Creamed Crab on Toast

NINA DE WITT • AURORA, OHIO

This is a great ready-in-a-jiffy luncheon dish or Sunday supper. The addition of marjoram and lemon juice in the sauce complements the flavor of the crab.

PREP/TOTAL TIME: 10 min.

1	can (10-3/4 ounces) condensed cream of mushroom soup, undiluted
1	can (6 ounces) crabmeat, rinsed, drained, and cartilage removed
1	tablespoon lemon juice
1/4	teaspoon dried marjoram

Dash cayenne pepper
Toast *or* biscuits

In a 1-qt. microwave-safe dish, combine the soup, crab, lemon juice, marjoram and cayenne. Cover and microwave on high for 3-4 minutes or until heated through, stirring once. Serve on toast or biscuits. YIELD: 4 SERVINGS.

EDITOR'S NOTE: This recipe was tested in a 1,100-watt microwave.

Bayou Country Seafood Casserole

ETHEL MILLER • EUNICE, LOUISIANA

Seafood is extremely popular in our area. Because crabs and shrimp are so plentiful in our bayous and rivers, they are used in a variety of recipes.

PREP: 35 min. **BAKE:** 30 min.

1	medium onion, chopped
1	medium green pepper, chopped
1	celery rib, chopped
1	garlic clove, minced
6	tablespoons butter
1	can (10-3/4 ounces) condensed cream of mushroom soup, undiluted
1	pound uncooked shrimp, peeled and deveined
1-1/2	cups cooked rice
2	cans (6 ounces *each*) crabmeat, drained, flaked and cartilage removed
4	slices day-old bread, cubed
3/4	cup half-and-half cream
1/4	cup chopped green onion tops
1/2	teaspoon salt
1/4	teaspoon pepper

Dash cayenne pepper

bayou country seafood casserole

TOPPING:

2	tablespoons butter, melted
1/3	cup dry bread crumbs
2	tablespoons snipped fresh parsley

In a large skillet, saute onion, green pepper, celery and garlic in butter until tender. Add soup and shrimp; cook and stir over medium heat 10 minutes or until shrimp turn pink. Stir in rice, crab, bread cubes, cream, onion tops and seasonings.

Spoon into a greased 2-qt. baking dish. Combine topping ingredients; sprinkle over casserole. Bake uncovered at 375° for 25-30 minutes or until the casserole is heated through. YIELD: 8 SERVINGS.

cooking tip

Convenient foil pouches of crabmeat are ready to use and don't require the hassle of removing any cartilage. You can easily use them in your recipes—just use two pouches for each 6-ounce can of crabmeat required in the recipe.

primavera fish fillets

Primavera Fish Fillets

CLARA COULSTON • WASHINGTON COURT HOUSE, OHIO

Tender cod fillets and fresh vegetables cook in a flavorful sauce that's easy to make with canned cream of mushroom soup. Since we're watching what we eat, I usually buy the lighter version of the soup.

PREP/TOTAL TIME: 25 min.

2	celery ribs, sliced
1	large carrot, cut into 2-inch julienne strips
1	small onion, chopped
1/4	cup water
2	tablespoons white wine *or* chicken broth
1/2	teaspoon dried thyme
1	can (10-3/4 ounces) condensed cream of mushroom soup, undiluted
1	pound frozen cod *or* haddock fillets, thawed

In a large skillet, combine the first six ingredients. Bring to a boil. Reduce heat; cover and simmer for 5-7 minutes or until vegetables are crisp-tender. Stir in soup until blended; bring to a boil. Add fillets. Reduce heat; cover and simmer for 5-7 minutes or until fish flakes easily with a fork. YIELD: 4 SERVINGS.

Creamy Seafood Casserole

MARY BROWN • WHITMAN, MASSACHUSETTS

I love this recipe I received from my mother. It's simple, tasty and can be made the night before for added convenience. The next day, all I have to do is pop it in the oven. Crushed potato chips make another yummy topping option.

PREP: 15 min. **BAKE:** 25 min.

1	pound flounder fillets, cut into 1-1/2-inch pieces
1	pound uncooked medium shrimp, peeled and deveined
1	can (10-3/4 ounces) condensed cream of shrimp soup, undiluted
1/4	cup milk
1	cup crushed butter-flavored crackers (about 25 crackers)
1/4	cup grated Parmesan cheese
1	teaspoon paprika
2	tablespoons butter, melted

Arrange fish and shrimp in a greased 11-in. x 7-in. x 2-in. baking dish. Combine soup and milk; pour over seafood. Combine the cracker crumbs, Parmesan cheese, paprika and butter; sprinkle over top. Bake, uncovered, at 350° for 25-30 minutes or until the fish flakes easily with a fork and the shrimp turn pink. YIELD: 6-8 SERVINGS.

Shrimp Rice Casserole

MARCIA URSCHEL • WEBSTER, NEW YORK

I've been making this delicious dish for more than 30 years, and it hasn't failed me once. It comes together quickly plus it always pleases family and friends.

PREP: 10 min. **BAKE:** 30 min.

12	ounces cooked medium shrimp, peeled and deveined
2	cups cooked rice
1	can (10-3/4 ounces) condensed cream of mushroom soup, undiluted
1	can (4 ounces) mushroom stems and pieces, drained
1	cup (4 ounces) shredded cheddar cheese
4	tablespoons butter, melted, *divided*
2	tablespoons chopped green pepper
2	tablespoons chopped onion

1	tablespoon lemon juice
1/2	teaspoon white pepper
1/2	teaspoon ground mustard
1/2	teaspoon Worcestershire sauce
1	cup soft bread crumbs

In a large bowl, combine the shrimp, rice, soup, mushrooms, cheese, 2 tablespoons butter, green pepper, onion, lemon juice, pepper, mustard and Worcestershire sauce.

Transfer to a greased 1-1/2-qt. baking dish. Combine bread crumbs and remaining butter; sprinkle over top. Bake, uncovered, at 375° for 30-35 minutes or until lightly browned. YIELD: 6 SERVINGS.

Saucy Dill Salmon Steaks

VALERIE HUTSON • BYRON, MINNESOTA

The moist salmon steaks and rich sauce are cooked in the same skillet for easy prep and cleanup. Friends have found this dinner to be elegant and delicious.

PREP/TOTAL TIME: 25 min.

1/2	cup chopped green onions
1	tablespoon butter
1	can (10-3/4 ounces) condensed cream of chicken soup, undiluted
1/2	cup half-and-half cream
2	tablespoons white wine *or* chicken broth
2	tablespoons chopped fresh dill *or* 2 teaspoons dill weed
4	salmon steaks (1 inch thick)

cooking tip

Overcooked fish loses its flavor and becomes tough. As a general guideline, fish is cooked 10 minutes for every inch of thickness. Here is an easy way to check for doneness: Insert a fork at an angle into the thickest portion of the fish and part the meat. When it is opaque and flakes into sections, the fish is cooked completely.

In a large skillet, saute the onions in butter. Add the soup, cream, wine or broth and dill. Place salmon steaks on top. Cover and simmer for 15 minutes or until fish flakes easily with a fork. YIELD: 4 SERVINGS.

Baked Shrimp & Asparagus

JANE RHODES • SILVERDALE, WASHINGTON

I invented this one-dish winner when I needed to serve 30 co-workers at a holiday party. It was such a hit, that now I make it frequently for guests. It tastes so special, yet it's fast to fix.

PREP/TOTAL TIME: 30 min.

1	package (12 ounces) frozen cut asparagus
1	pound uncooked medium shrimp, peeled and deveined
1	can (10-3/4 ounces) condensed cream of shrimp soup, undiluted
1	tablespoon butter, melted
1	teaspoon soy sauce
1/2	cup salad croutons, optional

Hot cooked rice

In a large bowl, combine the first five ingredients. Spoon into a greased 8-in. square baking dish.

Bake, uncovered, at 425° for 20 minutes or until shrimp turn pink. Top with croutons if desired; bake 5 minutes longer. Serve over rice. YIELD: 4-6 SERVINGS.

baked shrimp & asparagus

Pecan Salmon Casserole

EDNA COBURN • TUCSON, ARIZONA

Peas, pecans and pimientos complement the salmon in this potluck-perfect dish that's topped with crushed potato chips for an added crunch. I find the one-dish entree is great for family dinners, too.

PREP: 20 min. **BAKE:** 30 min.

1	package (16 ounces) small shell pasta
2	medium onions, finely chopped
1/2	pound sliced fresh mushrooms
1/4	cup butter, cubed
2	cans (10-3/4 ounces *each*) condensed cream of mushroom soup, undiluted
1-1/2	cups milk
2	teaspoons Worcestershire sauce
1	teaspoon salt
1/2	teaspoon pepper
2	cans (14-3/4 ounces *each*) salmon, drained, bones and skin removed
2	cups frozen peas
1	cup chopped pecans, toasted
1	jar (2 ounces) diced pimientos, drained
1/2	cup crushed potato chips

Cook pasta according to package directions. Meanwhile, in a large skillet, saute the onions and mushrooms in butter until tender. Stir in the soup, milk, Worcestershire sauce, salt and pepper until blended; bring to a boil. Remove from the heat.

Drain pasta. Add the pasta, salmon, peas, pecans and pimientos to the skillet. Transfer to a greased shallow 3-qt. baking dish.

Cover and bake at 350° for 30-35 minutes or until heated through. Sprinkle with potato chips. YIELD: 12 SERVINGS.

pecan salmon casserole

Seafood Lasagna

VIOLA WALMER • TEQUESTA, FLORIDA

Everyone seems to enjoy this pasta bake. I like that I can prepare it the day before and refrigerate it overnight. The next day, I just take it out of the fridge 30 minutes before popping it in the oven.

PREP: 15 min. **BAKE:** 50 min. + standing

3/4	cup chopped onion
2	tablespoons butter
1	package (8 ounces) cream cheese, cubed
1-1/2	cups (12 ounces) 4% cottage cheese
1	egg, lightly beaten
2	teaspoons dried basil
1	teaspoon salt
1/4	teaspoon pepper
1	can (10-3/4 ounces) condensed cream of shrimp soup, undiluted
1	can (10-3/4 ounces) condensed cream of mushroom soup, undiluted
1/2	cup white wine *or* chicken broth
1/2	cup milk
2	packages (8 ounces *each*) imitation crabmeat, flaked
1	can (6 ounces) small shrimp, rinsed and drained
9	lasagna noodles, cooked and drained
1/2	cup grated Parmesan cheese
3/4	cup shredded Monterey Jack cheese

In a large skillet, saute onion in butter until tender. Reduce heat. Add cream cheese; cook and stir until melted and smooth. Stir in the cottage cheese, egg, basil, salt and pepper. Remove from the heat and set aside. In a large bowl, combine the soups, wine or broth, milk, crab and shrimp.

Arrange three noodles in a greased 13-in. x 9-in. x 2-in. baking dish. Spread with a third of cottage cheese mixture and a third of the seafood mixture. Repeat layers twice. Sprinkle with Parmesan cheese.

Cover and bake at 350° for 40 minutes. Uncover; sprinkle with the Monterey Jack cheese. Bake 10 minutes longer or until cheese is melted and the lasagna is bubbly. Let stand for 15 minutes before serving. YIELD: 12 SERVINGS.

Mushroom Haddock Loaf

CRAIG BROWN • SIOUX CITY, IOWA

This savory loaf, which uses haddock, tastes very much like tuna casserole. I have made it several times for family and friends, and they all enjoy it.

PREP: 15 min. **BAKE:** 55 min.

1-1/2	cups crushed saltines (about 45 crackers)
1	can (10-3/4 ounces) condensed cream of mushrooms soup, undiluted
2	eggs, lightly beaten
1/3	cup milk
2	tablespoons chopped green onion
1	tablespoon lemon juice
2	drops hot pepper sauce
2	cups flaked cooked haddock

In a bowl, combine the cracker crumbs, soup, eggs, milk, onion, lemon juice and pepper sauce; mix well. Add the haddock. Press into a greased 8-in. x 4-in. x 2-in. loaf pan. Bake at 350° for 55-60 minutes or until a knife inserted near the center comes out clean. YIELD: 6 SERVINGS.

Broccoli Tuna Squares

JANET JUNCKER • GENEVA, OHIO

Those who try it always ask for this recipe because it's different from the traditional version. I make it when I don't have a lot of time to cook.

PREP: 15 min. **BAKE:** 35 min.

1	tube (8 ounces) refrigerated crescent rolls
1	cup (4 ounces) shredded Monterey Jack cheese
3	cups frozen chopped broccoli, cooked and drained
4	eggs
1	can (10-3/4 ounces) condensed cream of broccoli soup, undiluted
2	tablespoons mayonnaise
3/4	teaspoon onion powder
1/2	teaspoon dill weed
1	can (12 ounces) tuna, drained and flaked
1	tablespoon diced pimientos, drained

Unroll crescent roll dough into one long rectangle; place in an ungreased 13-in. x 9-in. x 2-in. baking

cheesy tuna mac

dish. Seal seams and perforations; press onto bottom and 1/2 in. up the sides. Sprinkle with cheese and broccoli. In a bowl, combine the eggs, soup, mayonnaise, onion powder and dill; mix well. Stir in tuna and pimientos; pour over broccoli.

Bake, uncovered, at 350° for 35-40 minutes or until a knife inserted near the center comes out clean. Let stand for 10 minutes before serving. YIELD: 8 SERVINGS.

Cheesy Tuna Mac

STEPHANIE MARTIN • MACOMB, MICHIGAN

What could be easier than dressing up a boxed macaroni and cheese mix with canned tuna and cream of broccoli soup? This comforting meal-in-one is a snap to prepare, and my two boys gobble it up. Feel free to vary the soup and veggies to suit your family's tastes.

PREP: 15 min. **BAKE:** 25 min.

1	package (7-1/2 ounces) macaroni and cheese mix
1/2	cup milk
1	tablespoon butter
1	can (10-3/4 ounces) condensed cream of broccoli soup, undiluted
1	can (6 ounces) tuna, drained and flaked
3/4	cup frozen peas
2	tablespoons finely chopped onion
1	tablespoon process cheese sauce

Cook the macaroni according to package directions; drain. Stir in the milk, butter and contents of cheese packet. Add the cream of broccoli soup, tuna, peas, onion and cheese sauce.

Spoon into a greased 1-1/2-qt. baking dish. Cover and bake at 350° for 20 minutes. Uncover; bake for 5-10 minutes longer or until casserole is heated through. YIELD: 4 SERVINGS.

CHAPTER 8
Sides

Creamy Pea Casserole

MARY PAULINE MAYNOR • FRANKLINTON, LOUISIANA

My sister-in-law shared this kid-friendly recipe with me a few years back. It is guaranteed to be a welcome addition to your dinner table.

PREP: 15 min. **BAKE:** 25 min.

- 1   medium onion, chopped
- 3   celery ribs, finely chopped
- 1/2   medium sweet red pepper, chopped
- 6   tablespoons butter
- 1   can (10-3/4 ounces) condensed cream of mushroom soup, undiluted
- 1   tablespoon milk
- 2   cups frozen peas, thawed
- 1   can (8 ounces) sliced water chestnuts, drained
- 1/2   to 3/4 cup crushed butter-flavored crackers (about 12 crackers)

In a skillet, saute the onion, celery and red pepper in butter for 8-10 minutes or until tender. Stir in the soup and milk; heat through. Stir in the peas and water chestnuts.

Transfer mixture to a greased 1-1/2-qt. baking dish. Sprinkle top with the cracker crumbs. Bake, uncovered, at 350° for 25-30 minutes or until casserole is bubbly. YIELD: 6 SERVINGS.

Corn 'n' Bean Bake

NELLIE PERDUE • ALBANY, KENTUCKY

Treat your family to a delicious surprise when you present this green bean dish with a twist. Adding whole kernel corn and buttery cracker crumbs brings a new taste to an heirloom recipe.

PREP: 10 min. **BAKE:** 35 min.

- 1   package (16 ounces) frozen cut green beans
- 1   can (15-1/4 ounces) whole kernel corn, drained
- 1   can (10-3/4 ounces) condensed cream of mushroom soup, undiluted
- 1   cup (4 ounces) shredded cheddar cheese, *divided*
- 1/2   cup crushed butter-flavored crackers (about 12 crackers)

In a bowl, combine the green beans, corn, soup and 1/2 cup cheese. Spoon into a greased 2-qt. baking dish. Top with cracker crumbs and remaining cheese. Bake, uncovered, at 350° for 35 minutes or until heated through. YIELD: 6 SERVINGS.

floret noodle bake

Floret Noodle Bake

TARA BRICCO • COVINGTON, TENNESSEE

I found the recipe for this vegetable casserole in an old magazine I bought at a yard sale soon after I was married. It has stood the test of time! Packed with veggies, it's a wonderful side dish for any meat entree.

PREP: 15 min. **BAKE:** 30 min.

- 1   can (10-3/4 ounces) condensed cream of mushroom soup, undiluted
- 1   cup (8 ounces) sour cream
- 3/4   cup chopped onion
- 1   teaspoon salt
- 1/4   teaspoon pepper
- 3   cups frozen chopped broccoli, thawed
- 1   package (8 ounces) frozen cauliflower, thawed and cut into bite-size pieces
- 8   ounces wide egg noodles, cooked and drained
- 1-1/2   cups (6 ounces) shredded Swiss cheese, *divided*

In a large bowl, combine the soup, sour cream, onion, salt and pepper. Add the broccoli, cauliflower, egg noodles and 1/4 cup of cheese; mix gently. Pour into a greased 13-in. x 9-in. x 2-in. baking dish. Top mixture with the remaining cheese. Bake, uncovered, at 350° for 30 minutes or until heated through. YIELD: 6-8 SERVINGS.

spinach supreme

Sausage Pilaf

KELLY MORRISSEY • OVERLAND PARK, KANSAS

I received this recipe from my mother years ago, and it's been a family treasure ever since. Pork sausage really bulks up ordinary rice pilaf.

PREP: 15 min. **BAKE:** 70 min.

1/2	pound bulk pork sausage
1	cup chopped celery
1/2	cup chopped onion
1/2	cup chopped green pepper
1	can (10-3/4 ounces) condensed cream of mushroom soup, undiluted
1-1/4	cups milk
1	jar (2 ounces) diced pimientos, drained
1/2	cup uncooked long grain rice
1/2	teaspoon poultry seasoning
1/4	teaspoon salt
1	cup soft bread crumbs
2	tablespoons butter, melted

In a skillet, cook sausage, celery, onion and green pepper until sausage is no longer pink and vegetables are tender; drain. Stir in soup, milk, pimientos, rice, poultry seasoning and salt.

Pour into an ungreased 1-1/2-qt. baking dish. Cover and bake at 350° for 50 minutes, stirring occasionally.

Combine bread crumbs and melted butter; sprinkle on top. Bake, uncovered, for 20 minutes longer. YIELD: 6-8 SERVINGS.

Spinach Supreme

CYNDI GAVIN • BLACKFOOT, IDAHO

This is the best spinach bake I have ever tasted! It's cheesy, delicious and so simple to make. I use the left-overs—if there are any—to make bite-size appetizer turnovers featuring phyllo dough.

PREP: 10 min. **BAKE:** 25 min.

2	packages (10 ounces *each*) frozen chopped spinach, thawed and squeezed dry
2	cups (8 ounces) shredded Monterey Jack cheese
1	can (10-3/4 ounces) condensed cream of potato soup, undiluted
1	cup (8 ounces) sour cream
1/2	cup grated Parmesan cheese

In a large bowl, combine all of the ingredients. Transfer to a greased 11-in. x 7-in. x 2-in. baking dish. Bake, uncovered, at 325° for 25-30 minutes or until the edges are lightly browned and bubbly. YIELD: 4-6 SERVINGS.

Mushroom Corn Bread Dressing

RUBY WILLIAMS • BOGALUSA, LOUISIANA

This rave-winning dressing is moist and flavorful, and it makes enough for a large gathering. Plus, it goes well with beef, chicken, turkey or ham.

PREP: 20 min. **BAKE:** 65 min.

2	cups cornmeal
3	teaspoons sugar
3	teaspoons baking powder
1	teaspoon salt
5	eggs
1	can (12 ounces) evaporated milk
1/4	cup vegetable oil
2	cups chopped fresh mushrooms
1	cup chopped celery
1/2	cup chopped green onions

3 tablespoons butter
2 cans (14-1/2 ounces *each*) chicken broth
1 can (10-3/4 ounces) condensed cream of chicken soup, undiluted
1/4 cup sliced almonds, toasted
1 teaspoon poultry seasoning
1/4 teaspoon pepper

For corn bread, combine the first four ingredients in a bowl. Combine 2 eggs, milk and oil; stir into dry ingredients just until moistened. Pour into a greased 9-in. square baking pan. Bake at 400° for 18-20 minutes or until a toothpick inserted near center comes out clean. Cool on a wire rack.

In a skillet, saute mushrooms, celery and onions in butter until tender. In a large bowl, beat remaining eggs. Add broth, soup, almonds, poultry seasoning, pepper and sauteed vegetables. Crumble corn bread over mixture.

Pour into a greased 13-in. x 9-in. x 2-in. baking dish. Bake, uncovered, at 350° for 45-50 minutes or until a knife comes out clean. YIELD: 10-12 SERVINGS.

Creamy Broccoli Casserole

CAROLYN CREASMAN • GASTONIA, NORTH CAROLINA

This home-style side dish is a scrumptious way to showcase broccoli. It's lovely on a buffet or anytime you want to make an ordinary meal extra special. I especially like serving it with chicken.

PREP: 10 min. **BAKE:** 25 min.

6 cups frozen chopped broccoli
2 eggs, lightly beaten
1 can (10-3/4 ounces) condensed cream of mushroom soup, undiluted
1 cup mayonnaise
1 cup (4 ounces) shredded cheddar cheese
1 small onion, finely chopped
1/2 cup butter, melted
1/3 cup crushed butter-flavored crackers (about 8 crackers)

Place 1 in. of water and broccoli in a large saucepan; bring to a boil. Reduce heat; cover and simmer for 5-8 minutes or until crisp-tender. Meanwhile, in a bowl, combine the eggs, soup, mayonnaise, cheese, onion and butter. Drain broccoli; gently stir into soup mixture.

Pour into a greased 2-qt. baking dish. Sprinkle with crushed cracker crumbs. Bake, uncovered, at 350° for 25-30 minutes or until heated through. YIELD: 9 SERVINGS.

Festive Green Bean Casserole

JUNE MULLINS • LIVONIA, MISSOURI

This recipe came from a cookbook my son gave me over 20 years ago. It's one I make often when I want a change from the traditional version.

PREP/TOTAL TIME: 30 min.

1 cup chopped sweet red pepper
1 small onion, finely chopped
1 tablespoon butter
1 can (10-3/4 ounces) condensed cream of celery soup, undiluted
1/2 cup milk
1 teaspoon Worcestershire sauce
1/8 teaspoon hot pepper sauce
2 packages (16 ounces *each*) frozen French-style green beans, thawed and drained
1 can (8 ounces) sliced water chestnuts, drained
1 cup (4 ounces) shredded cheddar cheese

In a skillet, saute red pepper and onion in butter until tender. Add soup, milk, Worcestershire sauce and hot pepper sauce; stir until smooth. Stir in beans and water chestnuts.

Transfer to an ungreased 1-1/2-qt. baking dish. Sprinkle with cheese. Bake, uncovered, at 350° for 15 minutes or until heated through. YIELD: 6-8 SERVINGS.

festive green bean casserole

Vegetable Macaroni

ELIZABETH ERWIN • SYRACUSE, NEW YORK

This casserole works equally well as a side dish or meatless entree. Even my meat-and-potatoes husband enjoys it, especially with a loaf of crusty French bread.

PREP: 10 min. **BAKE:** 30 min.

- 1   can (10-3/4 ounces) condensed cream of celery soup, undiluted
- 1   cup (8 ounces) sour cream
- 1/4   cup milk
- 1   tablespoon dried minced onion
- 1/2   teaspoon salt
- 1/8   teaspoon pepper
- 2   packages (16 ounces *each*) frozen mixed vegetables, thawed
- 4   ounces elbow macaroni, cooked and drained
- 2   cups (8 ounces) shredded cheddar cheese

In a large bowl, combine the soup, sour cream, milk, onion, salt and pepper. Stir in the vegetables, macaroni and cheese.

Transfer to a greased 3-qt. baking dish. Cover and bake at 375° for 30-35 minutes or until bubbly.
YIELD: 8 SERVINGS.

Parmesan Spinach and Noodles

MERRIE FISCHER • GLEN ARM, MARYLAND

I love this noodle dish because it is so quick to fix and very versatile. Sometimes I will dress it up by stirring in some cooked shrimp, crab, chicken or turkey for a more elegant-looking accompaniment.

PREP/TOTAL TIME: 30 min.

vegetable macaroni

- 6   ounces uncooked yolk-free noodles
- 1/2   cup chopped onion
- 1   package (10 ounces) frozen chopped spinach
- 1   can (10-3/4 ounces) reduced-fat reduced-sodium condensed cream of chicken soup, undiluted
- 4   ounces reduced-fat cream cheese, cubed
- 1/2   cup grated Parmesan cheese
- 1/3   cup fat-free milk
- 1/2   teaspoon dried parsley flakes
- 1/8   teaspoon dried basil
- 1/8   teaspoon ground nutmeg
- 1/8   teaspoon pepper

Cook noodles according to package directions. Meanwhile, place onion in a 2-qt. microwave-safe bowl. Cover and microwave on high for 3 minutes or until tender. Add spinach; cover and cook on high for 5 minutes or until spinach is thawed; stir.

Add the cream of chicken soup, cream cheese, Parmesan cheese, milk and seasonings; mix well. Cover and microwave at 50% power for 8 minutes or until heated through, stirring once. Drain noodles; add to spinach mixture and stir to coat.
YIELD: 5 SERVINGS.

EDITOR'S NOTE: This recipe was tested in an 850-watt microwave.

Hearty Vegetable Casserole

BILL COWAN • HANOVER, ONTARIO

This layered bake has lots of fall vegetables. It's gone to many potluck meals at our church. With a package of pork sausage in the recipe, you can serve 12 as a side dish or six as an all-in-one main course.

PREP: 15 min. **BAKE:** 1-1/2 hours

- 1   cup sliced turnips
- 1   cup diced carrots
- 1   cup diced potatoes
- 1   cup frozen peas
- 1   cup diced parsnips
- 1   cup shredded cabbage

Salt and pepper to taste

- 1   can (8 ounces) cut green beans
- 2   tablespoons chopped onion
- 1   package (12 ounces) fresh pork sausage links
- 1   can (10-3/4 ounces) condensed cream of mushroom soup, undiluted

In a greased 13-in. x 9-in. x 2-in. glass baking dish, layer the first six vegetables in order given, seasoning with salt and pepper between layers. Drain beans, reserving liquid; set liquid aside.

Place beans over cabbage; sprinkle with salt and pepper. Top with onion. Brown the sausage; drain. Place over onion. Combine soup and bean liquid; pour over sausage. Cover and bake at 350° for 1 hour. Turn sausage over; bake, uncovered, 30 minutes longer or until vegetables are tender. YIELD: 6 SERVINGS.

Calico Squash Casserole

LUCILLE TERRY • FRANKFORT, KENTUCKY

I try to find as many recipes as possible that use squash. It's a pleasure to present this colorful creation as part of a special-occasion menu.

PREP: 20 min. **BAKE:** 30 min.

2	cups sliced yellow summer squash (1/4 inch thick)
1	cup sliced zucchini (1/4 inch thick)
1	medium onion, chopped
1/4	cup sliced green onions
1	cup water
1	teaspoon salt, *divided*
2	cups crushed butter-flavored crackers (about 48 crackers)
1/2	cup butter, melted
1	can (10-3/4 ounces) condensed cream of chicken soup, undiluted
1	can (8 ounces) sliced water chestnuts, drained
1	large carrot, shredded
1/2	cup mayonnaise
1	jar (2 ounces) diced pimientos, drained
1	teaspoon rubbed sage
1/2	teaspoon white pepper
1	cup (4 ounces) shredded sharp cheddar cheese

In a large saucepan, combine the first five ingredients; add 1/2 teaspoon salt. Cover and cook until the squash is tender, about 6 minutes. Drain well; set aside.

Combine cracker crumbs and butter; spoon half into a greased shallow 1-1/2-qt. baking dish. In a large bowl, combine the soup, water chestnuts, carrot, mayonnaise, pimientos, sage, pepper and remaining salt; fold into squash mixture. Spoon over crumbs.

Sprinkle with cheese and the remaining crumb mixture. Bake, uncovered, at 350° for 30 minutes or until lightly browned. YIELD: 8 SERVINGS.

creamy red potatoes

Creamy Red Potatoes

SHELIA SCHMITT • TOPEKA, KANSAS

I know I can please a crowd with this rich and smooth potato casserole. It's very easy to double, and I've always received compliments when I've served it.

PREP: 5 min. **COOK:** 8 hours

2	pounds small red potatoes, quartered
1	package (8 ounces) cream cheese, softened
1	can (10-3/4 ounces) condensed cream of potato soup, undiluted
1	envelope ranch salad dressing mix

Place potatoes in a 3-qt. slow cooker. In a small mixing bowl, beat cream cheese, soup and salad dressing mix. Mix until blended. Stir into potatoes. Cover and cook on low for 8 hours or until potatoes are tender. YIELD: 4-6 SERVINGS.

cooking tip

If you don't have a garden to supply you with summer squash, buy firm squash with brightly colored skin that's free from spots and bruises. Generally, the smaller the squash, the more tender it will be.

corn-stuffed peppers

Corn-Stuffed Peppers

SUZANNE HUBBARD • GREELEY, COLORADO

I created this recipe and haven't had any complaints yet! The peppers can be served alone as a light meal or alongside pork chops, steak—even hamburgers.

PREP: 15 min. **BAKE:** 45 min.

4	medium green peppers
1	can (10-3/4 ounces) condensed cream of celery soup, undiluted
2-1/2	cups frozen loose-pack hash browns, thawed
2	cups fresh *or* frozen corn
1/2	cup shredded cheddar cheese
1/4	cup chopped onion
1	jar (2 ounces) chopped pimientos, drained
2	tablespoons snipped fresh chives
1/2	teaspoons salt

Slice tops off peppers and reserve; remove seeds. In a bowl, combine the remaining ingredients. Spoon filling into peppers and replace tops.

Place peppers in an 8-in. square baking dish; cover with foil. Bake peppers at 350° for 45-60 minutes. YIELD: 4 SERVINGS.

Cabbage Au Gratin

LINDA FUNDERBURKE • BROCKPORT, NEW YORK

This cheesy bake was a favorite with my 10 siblings and me. We thought Mom was the world's best cook and she always outdid herself on Sundays, when this popular dish was usually served!

PREP/TOTAL TIME: 30 min.

1	medium head cabbage, shredded (about 8 cups)
1	can (10-3/4 ounces) condensed cream of celery soup, undiluted
2	tablespoons milk
1	cup shredded process American cheese (Velveeta)
1	cup soft bread crumbs
1	tablespoon butter

In a large covered saucepan, cook cabbage in boiling salted water for 5 minutes; drain. Place in a greased 8-in. square baking dish.

In a small saucepan, blend soup and milk; heat well. Add cheese and stir until melted. Pour over cabbage. Saute bread crumbs in butter until golden; sprinkle over cabbage. Bake at 350° for 15-20 minutes or until heated through. YIELD: 8-10 SERVINGS.

Potato Herb Bread

DIANE HIXON • NICEVILLE, FLORIDA

No one ever suspects that a can of cream of potato soup is the secret ingredient in this soft and chewy bread. This golden loaf is a mouth-watering and attractive addition to any meal.

PREP: 20 min. + rising **BAKE:** 30 min.

2	packages (1/4 ounce *each*) active dry yeast
2	tablespoons sugar plus 1 teaspoon sugar, *divided*
1/2	cup warm water (110° to 115°)
1	can (10-3/4 ounces) condensed cream of potato soup, undiluted
1	cup hot water
1/2	cup nonfat dry milk powder
1/2	cup sour cream
1/2	cup snipped fresh chives
2	tablespoons butter, melted
2	teaspoons salt
1	teaspoon dried tarragon, crushed
6	to 6-1/2 cups all-purpose flour

In a small bowl, dissolve yeast and 1 teaspoon sugar in warm water. Let stand for 5 minutes.

In a large mixing bowl, combine the cream of potato soup and hot water. Stir in yeast mixture, milk powder, sour cream, chives, butter, salt, tarragon and remaining sugar. Mix well. Add enough flour to make a stiff dough.

Turn dough onto a floured surface; knead until smooth and elastic, about 6 to 8 minutes. Place in a greased bowl, turning once to grease top. Cover and let rise in warm place until doubled, about 1 hour.

Punch dough down. Divide dough in half. Shape dough in two loaves and place in greased 9-in. x 5-in. x 3-in. loaf pans. Cover and let dough rise until doubled, about 30 minutes. Bake at 400° for 30 minutes or until golden. YIELD: 2 LOAVES.

Broccoli Supreme

LUCY PARKS • BIRMINGHAM, ALABAMA

I really don't know how long I've had this recipe, but it has been an old standby in our family for quite some time. I've shared it with many friends, too.

PREP: 10 min. **BAKE:** 50 min.

2	tablespoons all-purpose flour
2	cans (10-3/4 ounces *each*) condensed cream of chicken soup, undiluted
1	cup (8 ounces) sour cream
1/2	cup grated carrot
2	tablespoons grated onion
1/2	teaspoon pepper
3	packages (10 ounces *each*) frozen broccoli cuts, thawed
1-1/2	cups crushed seasoned stuffing
1/4	cup butter, melted

In a large bowl, combine the flour, soup and sour cream. Stir in the carrot, onion and pepper. Fold in the broccoli.

Transfer to a greased 2-1/2-qt. baking dish. Combine stuffing and butter; sprinkle over top. Bake, uncovered, at 350° for 50-60 minutes or until bubbly and heated through. YIELD: 12 SERVINGS.

cooking tip

Speed up the prep time for Cabbage Au Gratin by purchasing a bag of shredded cabbage at the store instead of shredding it yourself. Get creative with the flavor by replacing the process cheese with cubed Brie. It will add a rich and buttery taste to the side dish.

Harvest Carrots

MARTY RUMMEL • TROUT LAKE, WASHINGTON

I make this hearty side quite often. Once in a while, I will add leftover turkey or chicken breasts to turn it into a satisfying and filling entree.

PREP: 15 min. **BAKE:** 30 min.

4	cups sliced carrots
2	cups water
1	medium onion, chopped
1/2	cup butter, *divided*
1	can (10-3/4 ounces) condensed cream of celery soup, undiluted
1/2	cup shredded cheddar cheese
1/8	teaspoon pepper
3	cups seasoned stuffing croutons

In a large saucepan, bring carrots and water to a boil. Reduce heat; cover and simmer for 5-8 minutes or until tender. Drain. In a small skillet, saute onion in 3 tablespoons butter until tender.

In a large bowl, combine the carrots, onion, soup, cheese and pepper. Melt remaining butter; toss with stuffing. Fold into carrot mixture.

Transfer to a greased 2-qt. baking dish. Cover and bake at 350° for 20 minutes. Uncover; bake for 10 minutes longer or until the stuffing is lightly browned. YIELD: 6 SERVINGS.

harvest carrots

Squash Bake

THELMA MEFFORD • WETUMKA, OKLAHOMA

Besides serving it at home, I have often carried this dish to church dinners. It's a delightfully different addition to any buffet table and has always received plenty of praise. I serve it alongside chicken.

PREP: 20 min. **BAKE:** 25 min.

8	cups sliced yellow squash (about 2 pounds)
1/2	cup chopped onion
3/4	cup shredded carrots
1/4	cup butter
1	can (10-3/4 ounces) condensed cream of chicken soup, undiluted
1/2	cup sour cream
2	cups herb stuffing croutons, *divided*

Cook squash in lightly salted boiling water for 3 to 4 minutes or until crisp-tender; drain well. In a skillet, saute onion and carrots in butter until tender.

Combine onion and carrots with soup, sour cream and 1-1/2 cups croutons. Add squash and mix lightly. Spoon into a lightly greased 12-in. x 8-in. x 2-in. baking dish or a 2-qt. casserole. Sprinkle with the remaining croutons.

Bake, uncovered, at 350° for 25 minutes or until heated through. YIELD: 8-10 SERVINGS.

mushroom potatoes

Mushroom Potatoes

SKIP DOLLIVER • SOUTH HAMILTON, MASSACHUSETTS

I like serving this lighter alternative to average mashed potatoes. Our son thinks it is absolutely delicious and asks for it frequently.

PREP: 10 min. **BAKE:** 30 min.

1	can (10-3/4 ounces) reduced-fat reduced-sodium condensed cream of mushroom soup, undiluted
1/2	cup fat-free milk
1	large onion, chopped
4	medium potatoes, peeled, diced and cooked
	Paprika

In a bowl, combine soup, milk and onion. Stir in the potatoes. Pour into a 1-1/2-qt. baking dish that has been coated with cooking spray. Sprinkle top with paprika. Bake, uncovered, at 350° for 30 minutes or until bubbly. YIELD: 8 SERVINGS.

Creamy Hash Browns

SHIRLEY KIDD • NEW LONDON, MINNESOTA

No one will ever guess these saucy potatoes are a good-for-you side dish. So rich and cheesy, they can accompany just about any main course.

PREP: 5 min. **BAKE:** 50 min.

1	package (28 ounces) frozen O'Brien hash brown potatoes
1	cup (4 ounces) shredded reduced-fat cheddar cheese
1	can (4 ounces) chopped green chilies

squash bake

- 1 can (10-3/4 ounces) reduced-fat reduced-sodium condensed cream of chicken soup, undiluted
- 1 cup (8 ounces) reduced-fat sour cream

In a large bowl, combine the potatoes, cheese and chilies. Transfer to a 13-in. x 9-in. x 2-in. baking dish coated with cooking spray. Combine soup and sour cream; spread evenly over potato mixture. Bake, uncovered, at 350° for 50-55 minutes or until potatoes are tender. YIELD: 10 SERVINGS.

Corn Bread Veggie Bake

SHARON VAN ORNUM • HILTON, NEW YORK

I take advantage of convenience items in this simple creation that's very inexpensive. The veggie-packed specialty is great with any menu.

PREP: 10 min. **BAKE:** 25 min.

- 1 can (10-3/4 ounces) condensed cream of mushroom soup, undiluted
- 1 cup milk, *divided*
- 1-1/2 cups frozen mixed vegetables, thawed
- 1 package (8-1/2 ounces) corn bread/muffin mix
- 1 egg, lightly beaten
- 2/3 cup French-fried onions

In a large bowl, combine soup, 2/3 cup milk and vegetables. Transfer vegetable mixture to a greased 11-in. x 7-in. x 2-in. baking dish. In a large bowl, combine the corn bread mix, egg and remaining milk just until blended. Carefully spread over vegetable mixture.

Sprinkle with French-fried onions (pan will be full). Bake at 350° for 25-30 minutes or until lightly browned and a toothpick inserted near the center comes out clean. YIELD: 6 SERVINGS.

cooking tip

Onions are low in calories but high in taste. They're also a good source of potassium. In fact, 1/2 cup of chopped onion yields about 240 mg of potassium, similar to 1/2 banana or 1/2 cup of orange juice.

cheesy onion casserole

Cheesy Onion Casserole

BETH PERRY • JACKSONVILLE, FLORIDA

If you like French onion soup, you'll adore my oven-baked version. It serves up the mouth-watering flavor of the soup in a pleasing casserole. I think it pairs well with a Sunday beef roast dinner.

PREP: 15 min. **BAKE:** 30 min.

- 2 tablespoons butter
- 3 large sweet onions, sliced
- 2 cups (8 ounces) shredded Swiss cheese, *divided*
- Pepper to taste
- 1 can (10-3/4 ounces) condensed cream of chicken soup, undiluted
- 2/3 cup milk
- 1 teaspoon soy sauce
- 8 slices French bread, buttered on both sides

In a large skillet, melt butter. Saute onions until translucent and slightly brown. Layer the onions and two-thirds of the swiss cheese in a 2-qt. baking dish, sprinkling pepper between layers.

In a saucepan, heat soup, milk and soy sauce; stir to blend. Pour over onions and stir gently. Top with bread. Bake, uncovered, at 350° for 15 minutes. Push bread under sauce; sprinkle with remaining cheese. Bake 15 minutes longer. YIELD: 8 SERVINGS.

creamy vegetable casserole

Potatoes Supreme

MRS. AFTON JOHNSON • SUGAR CITY, IDAHO

Hailing from the state known for its potatoes, I thought I'd share this recipe. Every time my grandson comes for a visit, he asks me to make it. In fact, it's the whole family's favorite potato dish.

PREP: 35 min. + cooling BAKE: 25 min.

  8   to 10 medium potatoes, peeled and cubed
  1   can (10-3/4 ounces) condensed cream of chicken soup, undiluted
  3   cups (12 ounces) shredded cheddar cheese, *divided*
  1   cup (8 ounces) sour cream
  3   green onions, chopped
Salt and pepper to taste

Place potatoes in a saucepan and cover with water. Bring to a boil; cover and cook until almost tender. Drain and cool. In a large bowl, combine soup, 1-1/2 cups cheese, sour cream, onions, salt and pepper; stir in potatoes.

    Place in a greased 13-in. x 9-in. x 2-in. baking dish. Sprinkle with remaining cheese. Bake, uncovered, at 350° for 25-30 minutes or until heated through. YIELD: 8-10 SERVINGS.

Creamy Vegetable Casserole

TAMI KRATZER • WEST JORDAN, UTAH

Searching for a different way to prepare veggies? Look no further. I have a fussy eater in my house who absolutely loves this medley. I appreciate that it can be assembled in a snap, leaving time to fix the main course, set the table or just sit back and relax.

PREP: 15 min. BAKE: 25 min.

  1   package (16 ounces) frozen broccoli, carrots and cauliflower
  1   can (10-3/4 ounces) condensed cream of mushroom soup, undiluted
  1   carton (8 ounces) spreadable garden vegetable cream cheese
1/2   to 1 cup seasoned croutons

Prepare vegetables according to package directions; drain and place in a large bowl. Stir in soup and cream cheese. Transfer to a greased 1-qt. baking dish. Sprinkle with croutons. Bake, uncovered, at 375° for 25 minutes or until bubbly. YIELD: 6 SERVINGS.

Ranch Potatoes

ELAINE EAVENSON • MOSELLE, MASSACHUSETTS

I sometimes substitute cream of chicken soup for the cream of mushroom soup I usually use in this recipe. Even the "particular eaters" in my family love these potatoes.

PREP: 20 min. BAKE: 25 min.

  8   to 10 medium potatoes, peeled and cut into 1/2-inch cubes
  1   can (10-3/4 ounces) condensed cream of mushroom soup, undiluted

cooking tip

Keep extra cooked rice on hand for recipes like Broccoli with Rice. On the weekend, cook a good-size pot. Having it in the refrigerator will help you get dinner on the table quicker during the week!

broccoli with rice

1-1/4   cups milk
1   envelope ranch salad dressing mix
1-1/4   cups (5 ounces) shredded sharp cheddar cheese, *divided*
Salt and pepper to taste
6   bacon strips, cooked and crumbled

Place potatoes in a saucepan and cover with water. Bring to a boil; cook potatoes until almost tender, about 10 minutes. Drain; place in a greased 13-in. x 9-in. x 2-in. baking dish.

Combine soup, milk, salad dressing mix, 1 cup cheese, salt and pepper; pour over potatoes. Top with bacon and remaining cheese. Bake, uncovered, at 350° for 25-30 minutes or until the potatoes are tender. YIELD: 10 SERVINGS.

Broccoli with Rice

SONDRA OSTHEIMER • BOSCOBEL, WISCONSIN

This easy stovetop specialty is a real time-saver because it takes advantage of cooked rice and canned cream of mushroom soup. And unlike other sides, there aren't a lot of vegetables to cut up. I've found that when prepared this way, kids are sure to eat all of their veggies.

PREP/TOTAL TIME: 20 min.

1   package (16 ounces) frozen broccoli cuts
1-1/2   cups cooked rice
1   can (10-3/4 ounces) condensed cream of mushroom soup, undiluted

In a saucepan, cook broccoli according to package directions; drain. Add rice and soup. Cook until heated through. YIELD: 4 SERVINGS.

Special Brussels Sprouts

RUBY MIGUEZ • CROWLEY, LOUISIANA

I grew up on a farm in southern Louisiana, so we had fresh vegetables most of the year. Mother served brussels sprouts at least twice a week. Fresh from the garden, they were sweet and tender. Now I make this recipe all year using frozen sprouts.

PREP/TOTAL TIME: 15 min.

1/4   cup sliced almonds
1   tablespoon butter
1   package (16 ounces) frozen brussels sprouts
1   chicken bouillon cube
1   can (10-3/4 ounces) condensed cream of chicken soup, undiluted
2   tablespoons milk
1   jar (2 ounces) chopped pimientos, drained
1/4   teaspoon pepper
1/8   teaspoon dried thyme

In a small skillet, saute almonds in butter until lightly browned; set aside. In a saucepan, cook brussels sprouts according to package directions, adding the bouillon cube to the water.

Meanwhile, in another saucepan, combine the soup, milk, pimientos, pepper and thyme. Cook until heated through. Drain sprouts; top with the cream sauce and stir gently. Sprinkle with almonds. YIELD: 4-6 SERVINGS.

special brussels sprouts

General Recipe Index

Alphabetical Index